Spanish for Gay Men

Spanish that was never taught in the classroom!

jonathan l. charles

T0365553

iUniverse, Inc.
Bloomington

Spanish for Gay Men
Spanish that was never taught in the classroom!

iUniverse books may be ordered through booksellers or by contacting:

iUniverse
1663 Liberty Drive
Bloomington, IN 47403
www.iuniverse.com
1-800-Authors (1-800-288-4677)

ISBN: 978-1-4697-5270-9 (sc)
ISBN: 978-1-4697-5271-6 (e)

Printed in the United States of America

iUniverse rev. date: 2/20/2012

Spanish for Gay Men

Spanish that was never taught in the classroom!

Academic and enrichingly enticing !

*Spanish Pronunciation Guide
   *Basic Spanish Structure with an erotic twist
*English to Spanish, ABC's
   How to express your wants and desires.

*Expressions of Love and terms of endearment

*Erotic Situations, Spanish to English ABC's Getting dirty

And much more!!!

TABLE OF CONTESTS

Introduction

This book is not designed as a teaching tool, but rather a book to 'enlighten' the user to the colorful usage of Spanish of the gay male traveler, of internet use, as well as to learn 'what is not taught' in the academic classroom setting. It does not attempt to teach the structure of Spanish but instead to help you express most everything that you would like, while in the gay Latino community or in the many exciting Spanish speaking countries.

The **Pronunciation Guide** should help the non-language person in the erotic usage with interesting and exciting practical situations. There are many useful examples that will enhance your language usage. The pronunciation guide will stress the Latin American pronunciation with explanations of the Castilian usage.

The **Structural Section** of the book will be a guide to the many ways you are able to enrich the usage of the language. Selected tenses being used will be practical for your purpose as well as a brief explanation of other important structural concepts will be explained.

The **ABC** sections of the book not only includes most every word that you may wish to use in English with the Spanish equivalent, but also provides ample examples of the usage of these expressions in a very practical manner. In these sections of the book most all words will be introduced with examples of their usage; the natural stressed vowel will be underscored to assist you with the correct pronunciation and after you get the idea the underscored stressed syllable will be discontinued.

The **Phrase Section** of the book is designed to present you with varied situations with important basic expressions that are of importance in language usage. Included will also be a section of body parts and a conversation table to the metric system, around the house and city, important everyday expressions, places to go and things to see.

The **last ABC** section of the book is from Spanish to English which includes 'the dirty words' in Spanish, and how they may be used regardless of the country. Some expressions may not have the same meaning from one country to the next, but it will be understood; so be careful with their usages. As you will find, many expressions may cause serious trouble. Many times, things are better not spoken.

Another section is **Understanding 'Machismo'** in the gay community and the many misconceptions of the term *Macho*. The **Latino World** section will be *a reference guide concerning gay life in the many Spanish speaking countries.* Be aware that some countries are more developed and have a greater acceptance of gay men as well as lesbian women. Spain and Argentina are in the mainstream with other countries not far behind. Being aware of the many cultural differences, customs and traditions as well as the laws of the different countries are extremely important.

After years of study and travel in many Spanish speaking countries, interviewing many men, and teaching Spanish at the high school and university levels, **I have found that this book is way overdue.** The academics of Spanish are very important but, *the contents of the book consists of what many have wanted to know and have never been taught.* Well, it is finally here!

The focus is on what you have always wanted to express but were unable. This book is complete and may be used for reference as well as study. The phrases and vocabulary are applicable for usage in the Spanish speaking countries without making reference to local dialect or country differences.

It is my hope that you start at the beginning of the book and then continue to the many chapters that will guide you to a better understanding of *colorful and erotic* Spanish, but that is not necessary if you have studied the language previously. **Start where ever you would like and enjoy the enrichment!**

JLC

Guide

for

Spanish

Pronunciation

Spanish Pronunciation Guide

For the most part, Spanish is phonetic and this guide for pronunciation will be made as easy as possible for you. So enjoy and learn.

The vowel sounds are pure:

A   "ah"   as in the English word that cheerleaders use:

Rah Rah

Spanish word = **mamar**-to suck

                casa-house

                cama-bed

E   "eh"   as in the Canadian expression:

Eh?

Spanish word = **Pepe**

                deme-give me

I   "ee"   as in the English word: tree

Spanish word = **para ti**=for you

The **Y** has the same sound as the **I**

O   "oh"   as in the English word: tow (short sound)

Spanish word = **puto**-male whore/bitch

U   "oo"   as in the English word: truth

Spanish word = **pu̲tear**-to whore around/to bitch

U and **I** are weak vowel sounds and when combined with other vowels they do not get as much stress.

A, **E** and **O** are the strong vowels sounds and get more stress when combined with other vowel sounds.

Combined vowel sounds may include:

ua   as in the Chinese word: "wo̲nton soup"

Spanish word = **agu̲a**-water

ue   as in the English word: way

Spanish word = **bu̲e̲no**-good/ok

ui   as in the Australian fruit: ke̲wi̲

Spanish word = **cu̲i̲dar**-to take care of

uo   as in the cowboy expression: "*woo* ther hurse"

Spanish word = **mutu̲o̲**= mutual

Special combinations of letters:

que = will always be pronounced as "kay"

qui = will always be pronounced as "key"

gue = will always be pronounced as "gay"

gui = will always be pronounced as the "gu̲i̲ in guion (script)"

*There are few differences in the consonants and most have similar sounds, but **soften** them.*

7

These are a few special consonants:

The **V** and the **B** are pronounced the same

<u>V</u>oy (boy)- I am going

<u>B</u>esar- to kiss

The double **RR** has a little trill

Bu<u>rr</u>o (as in row)- donkey

The **Ch** sound which may be considered as one letter

Mu<u>ch</u>a<u>ch</u>o-boy

Mu<u>ch</u>o-much/a lot

The doble **LL** has the sound of the "ya"

Se <u>ll</u>ama-His name is ...

No <u>ll</u>ores-Don't cry

The **Ñ** has the sound as the "<u>oni</u>on/ca<u>ny</u>on)

Sue<u>ñ</u>o contigo-I dream about you

Se<u>ñ</u>or-sir/Mr.

No me hagas da<u>ñ</u>o-Don't hurt me

The **H** is written but *not pronounced*!

Hacer el amor-to make love

Let's look at the alphabet.
To pronounce each consonant, a vowel sound is also used, some before and or after the consonant, others may have a guide to pronounce in parenthesis to help with each sound for pronunciation.

A   Be   Ce   Che   De   *E*   eFe   Ge (as in the word 'hay')

H(ache)   *I*   J(ota)(the J as an H sound and the *wha* sound in the word 'What'/and with 'Who'')

Ka   eLe   eLLe   eMe   eNe   eÑe   *O*   Pe
Q (cu)

eRe   eRRe   eSe   Te   *U*   Ve   W(doble U o V)
Y griega   Zeta

Note:
The **C** before *E* and *I* will have an '*s*' sound ….and a <u>strong</u> '*ka*' sound before *O, U* and *A*.

> **C**inco pulgadas.= Five inches.

> ¿**Có**mo se llama? = What is your name?

The **G** before *E* and *I* will have an '*hay/he*' sound…. and a <u>strong</u> '*ga/go/gu*' sound before *O, U* and *A*.

> **Ge**raldo es mi ami**go**.-Geraldo is my friend.

> Ten**ga** buena noche.-Have a good evening/night.

9

There are very few words that begin with **K** and **W**, most are from another language. Also if you have been to a Mexican restaurant and or a Taco Bell, remember how many of those food items are pronounced. Smiles !

There are only 2 rules for pronouncing Spanish words with only one exception.

1. If the word ends in a vowel (*A, E, I, O and U*) or the letters "*N*" or "*S*" == the *natural stress* is on *the next to the last syllable*. Most syllables consist of a consonant and a vowel.

Mamo	I suck
Follo	I fuck
Tra**ba**jo	I work
Polla	cock/dick (Spain)
Verga	cock/dick (Latin America)

2. If the word ends with any other consonant other than "n" or "s"== **the *natural stress* is on *the last syllable*.**

Be**sar**	to kiss
Chu**par**	to suck
Ma**mar**	to suck
Co**ger**	to fuck (Latin America)
Fo**llar**	to fuck (Spain)
Natu**ral**	natural

The only exception is a WRITTEN accent mark, which means that you stress that vowel which is accented. See the accent, then pronounce it! Great!

Cógeme	Fuck me
Mámame	Suck me
Fóllame	Fuck me
Chúpame	Suck me
Bésame	Kiss me
Cogiéndote	Fucking you
Vas a chupármela	You are going to suck me off.

There are many words in English that are the same in Spanish but are not pronounced that same, be careful with them. Most words in English that end in TION ends in CIÓN in Spanish. Many words that end in TY and LY end in DAD and TAD in Spanish. There are many *cognates* that do mean what the sound like, but don't be mislead.

action = acción(first C has a K sound)liberty = libertad

direction = dirección

cruelty = crueldad

nation = nación

humanity = humanidad

ocean = océano

airplane = aeroplano

civil = civil

Guide
For
Spanish
Structure

with
an

Erotic Twist

Spanish Structure

A little bit of Spanish structure!

In this section of the handbook, I will only focus on the I, YOU, HE and the WE concepts. I will introduce all forms at the beginning to give an idea of the total structure.

In Spanish there are 6 verbal forms and the subject pronouns that correspond with the verbal endings. Let's begin with the many different subject pronouns.

YO	I
TÚ	You (someone you know well)
US̲TED **(Ud.)**	You (the formal You, for someone who you do not know or may be older or for whom you have respect)
ÉL	He
E̲LLA	She
NOS̲OTROS	WE
NOS̲OTRAS	We (feminine form)

Vosotros	You (familiar-plural you, used in Spain)
Vosotras	You familiar-plural-feminine-used in Spain)
ELLOS	They (masculine, which also includes females)
USTEDES (Uds.)	You (plural-you all)

Many times in Spanish we do not use the Subject pronouns, sometimes for clarity and emphasis. As you will see the verbal ending indicates who the speaker is or whom is doing the action. You will see this on the next page.

Buena Aventura = a good adventure to you

Remember, I am only concentrating on the **I, YOU, HE** and the **WE** forms

In Spanish, we have 3 types of infinitives **AR, ER** and **IR.**
Present Tense-for regular verbs. I will use irregulars throughout the book, not to worry.

AR infinitives take the following endings:

Yo	**O**	Nosotros	**AMOS**
Tú	**AS**	Vosotros	**áis**
Ud.	**A**	Uds.	**AN**

Note: the él, ella, usted and a person's name take the same ending **A**. The ellos, ellas, ustedes and persons names take the same ending **AN**

ER infinitives take the following endings:

Yo	**O**	Nosotros	**EMOS**
Tú	**ES**	Vosotros	**éis**
Ud.	**E**	Uds.	**EN**

Note: the él, ella, usted and a person's name take the same ending **E**. The ellos, ellas, ustedes and persons names take the same ending **EN**

IR infinitives take the following endings:

Yo	**O**	Nosotros	**EMOS**
Tú	**ES**	Vosotros	**ís**
Ud.	**E**	Uds.	**EN**

Note: the él, ella, usted and a person's name take the same ending **E**

The ellos, ellas, ustedes and persons' names take the same ending **EN**

As you see the ending indicates the subject, which will be applied very soon. In order to make an infinitive active, we must *drop* the **AR, ER** or the **IR** and then *add* the appropriate endings. Let us now look at making some infinitive active. I will not be using the subject pronouns in Spanish; I will only be using the verb forms.

Pues, amigos …. Vamos = Well, friends…. Let's go.

venir(drop the ir/irregular forms) to come

Vengo	I come (cum)(am coming)
Vienes	You come (are coming)
Viene	He comes (is coming)
Venimos	We come (are coming)

correrse(drop the er and change the se-note)

Me corro	I come (cum) (am coming)
Te corres	You come (are coming)
Se corre	He comes (is coming
Nos corremos	We come (are coming

Follar (drop the ar)

Follo	I fuck
Follas	You fuck
Folla	He fucks
Follamos	We fuck

Coger(drop the er)

Cojo	I fuck
Coges	You fuck
Coge	He fucks
Cogemos	We fuck

Mama<u>r</u>(drop the ar)

Mamo	I suck
Mamas	You suck
Mama	He sucks
Mamamos	We suck

Chupa<u>r</u>(drop the ar)

Chupo	I suck
Chupas	You suck
Chupa	He sucks
Chupamos	We suck

Lame<u>r</u>(drop the er)

Lamo	I lick/rim
Lames	You lick/rim
Lame	He licks/rims
Lamemos	We lick/rim

Besar(drop the ar)

Beso	I kiss
Besas	You kiss
Besa	He kisses
Besamos	We kiss

Abrazar(drop the ar)

Abrazo	I hug
Abrazas	You hug
Abraza	He hugs
Abrazamos	We hug

I hope you are getting the idea now... wow... *Me gusta usar estos verbos* = I like using these verbs .

And yes, remember that I have underscored the syllable to be stressed. *¡Qué bien!* = How nice
I hope that you have the idea for the Present Tense regular verbs. So, when you see verbals that end in **AR, ER** and **IR** you have some understanding as to what you are to do to make them active.

Now, for the _Definite Past Tense_ (el pretérito); you drop the AR, ER and IR and you add the following endings.

AR		**IR/ER**		**AR**	**IR/ER**
Yo	**é**	**í**	Nosotros	**amos**	**imos**
Tú	**aste**	**iste**	Vosotros	asteis	isteis
Él	**ó**	**ió**	Ellos	aron	ieron

Follar		
	Follé	I fucked
	Follaste	You fucked
	Folló	He fucked
	Follamos	We fucked

18

Chupar	Chupé	I sucked
	Chupaste	You sucked
	Chupó	He sucked
	Chupamos	We sucked
Coger	Cogí	I fucked
	Cogiste	You fucked
	Cogió	He fucked
	Cogimos	We fucked
Mamar	Mamé	I sucked
	Mamaste	You sucked
	Mamó	He sucked
	Mamamos	We sucked

I know you have the idea for the regular Definite Past Tense. Let's continue!

Another past tense is the **Imperfect Past** (el imperfecto) which expresses a continuance action or repeated action the past. It has a translation of **used to** or **was ____ing**. There are only 3 irregular verbs in this tense, wish I will include in this section. Of course, you know that you have to drop the **AR, ER** and the **IR** and then attach the following ending.

	AR	IR/ER		AR	IR/ER
Yo	aba	ía	Nosotros	ábamos	amos
Tú	abas	ías	Vosotros	abáis	íais
Él	aba	ía	Ellos	aban	ían

19

The *three irregulars* are listed below

Ser- to be

Yo	<u>e</u>ra	I was/used to be
Tú	<u>e</u>ras	You were/used to be
Él	<u>e</u>ra	He was/ used to be
Nos.	**éramos**	We were/used to be
Vos.	érais	You were/used to be (in Spain)
Ellos	eran	They were/used to be

Ir- to go

Yo	**<u>i</u>ba**	I used to go/was going
Tú	**<u>i</u>bas**	You used to go/were going
Él	**<u>i</u>ba**	He used to go /was going
Nos.	**<u>í</u>bamos**	We used to go /were going
Vos.	ibais	You used to go/were going
Ellos	iban	They used to go/ were going

Ver- to see

Yo	**ve<u>ía</u>**	I used to see/was seeing
Tú	**ve<u>ía</u>s**	You used to see/were seeing
Él	**ve<u>ía</u>**	He used to see/was seeing
Nos.	**ve<u>ía</u>mos**	We used to see/were seeing
Vos.	veíais	You used to see/were seeing
Ellos	veían	They used to see/were seeing

Now, some important *Imperfect Past* verbs that you will enjoy.

Follar	Yo	**follaba**	I used to fuck/was fucking
	Tú	**follabas**	You used to fuck/were fucking
	Él	**follaba**	He used to fuck/was fucking
	Nos.	**follábamos**	We used to fuck/were fucking

Coger	Yo	**cogía**	I used to fuck/was fucking
	Tú	**cogías**	You used to fuck/were fucking
	Él	**cogía**	He used to fuck/was fucking
	Nos.	**cogíamos**	We used to fuck/were fucking

Correrse-

Yo   **me coria**-I used to come(cum)/was coming

Tú   **te corrías**   You used to come/were coming

Él   **se corría**   He used to come/was coming

Nos.   **nos corríamos** We used to come/were coming

Let us look at expressing the *ING* in Spanish. Remember that we will also drop the **AR, ER** and the **IR** before we add the following endings. For the **AR**, we drop the **AR** and add *ANDO* and for the **ER** and **IR**, we drop the **ER** and **IR** and add *IENDO.* These ending give us the *ING* meaning in English. Now, let's look at many useful words and their formation.

You may notice that there may be some irregular forms. Don't' worry. *¿Estás listo?* = Are you ready? **Sí, estoy listo** = Yes, I am ready

Follar	**follando**	fucking
Coger	**cogiendo**	fucking
Chupar	**chupando**	sucking
Mamar	**mamando**	sucking
Acabar	**acabando**	coming
Venir	**viniendo**	coming
Correrse	**corriendo(se)**	coming
Abrazar	**abrazando**	hugging
Besar	**besando**	kissing
Lamer	**lamiendo**	licking/rimming

Great now that we know how to form these *ING* words or *gerunds*, let's use them. We use these gerunds with a helping verbal and that is the important verb **ESTAR** (to be). Let's look at it for a moment. We use the verbal to express: health conditions/temporary conditions and direction or location. The following are the forms.

Estar

Estoy	I am
Estás	You are
Está	He is
Estamos	We are
Estáis	You are
Están	They are

22

Now, we use the forms of **Estar** with the *ING* words or *gerunds*. Let's see!

Es**toy chupando**	I am sucking
Est**ás chupando**	You are sucking
Est**á chupando**	He is sucking
Est**amos chupando**	We are sucking

Estoy besa**ndo**	I am kissing
Est**ás be**sa**ndo**	You are kissing
Est**á be**sa**ndo**	He is kissing
Est**amos be**sa**ndo**	We are kissing

Enough with the tenses for the moment. Ok? What about **ME, YOU, HIM** and **US** as *object*s. Well, let's look!

Me	**ME**
You	**TE**
Him/it	**LO**
Us	**NOS**

Ok, now what? First we are going to attach these objects to an infinitive. Hold on tight, this could be interesting. *Vamos.* = *Let's go*

I want to fuck you.	**Quiero coger*te*.**
I want to suck you.	**Quiero ma*mar*te.**
I want to kiss you.	**Quiero be*sar*te.**
I want to hug you.	**Quiero abra*zar*te.**

23

I would like to know/meet him-**Me gustaría conocer*lo*.**

I would like to fuck him	**Me gustaría follar*lo*.**
I would like to fuck him	**Me gustaría coger*lo*.**
I would like to rim/lick him	**Me gustaría lamer*lo*.**

Do you want to know me?	**¿Quieres conocer*me*?**
Do you want to kiss me?	**¿Quieres besar*me*?**
Do you want to fuck me ?	**¿Quieres follar*me*?**
Do you want to suck me?	**¿Quieres mamar*me*?**

I hope you remember how the *qui* is pronounced, yes? A little hint = as in the English word "*key*" and the *e* sound = "*eh*" plus the "*row*" sound for "*ro*" give so the word *QUIERO* - I want.
*Ah**o**ra, lo **tengo**. = Now I have it.*

What about making phrase negative? No problem, place *No* before the verb form. Let's look as some good examples:

I don't fuck	*No* **follo**
He doesn't fuck	**Él** *no* **folla**
I don't kiss	*No* **beso**
He doesn't suck	**Él** *no* **mama**

We don't want to hug.	*No* **queremos abrazar.**
We are not fucking now	*No* **estamos follando ahora.**
You aren't coming now	*No* **estás viniendo ahora.**
You aren't fucking me now	*No* **estás cogiéndome ahora.**

Don't you want to kiss me?	¿*No* **qui_eres** be**sar**me?
Don't you want to fuck me	¿*No* **qui_eres** co**ger**me?
Doesn't he want to hug me	¿*No* **qui_ere** (él) **abra_zar**me?

¡**Qué bueno amigos!** – Great my friends. Now, what if you want to tell someone *what to do* or *not to do*? This is the **Imperative** or the **Command**. The commands we will use here are: *familiar and formal*- familiar for someone you know well, like you best friend or a newly made friend, sounds nice; and now the formal command. It's not too complicated. *Vamos a ver. – Let's see.* In much of our life we use commands: *do this, do that, don't do this , don't do that, let's do something, let's not do something…* wow.. Yes, it is true. Let's see the Commands.

To express the **polite/familiar command** to someone you know:
> Use the *Usted or Él* form of the present tense. Ok?

Infinitive-*You(tú)* form present tense
The Command:

Hablar Ud. habla(you speak/talk)	**ha**bla	= speak or talk
Follar Ud. folla(you fuck)	**fo**lla	= fuck
Mamar Ud. fama(you suck)	**ma**ma	= suck
Lamer Ud. lame(you lick/rim)	**la**me	= rim/lick

Now let's put and object with them. Note, there is an accent mark on the natural stress before we attach the object. *Bien Chévere - Real Cool*

Affirmative Commands   *Negative Commands* (a

few changes, note: there is not an accent mark and there is a little change in spelling of this command)

Háblame.-Talk to me. **No me hables.** Don't talk to me.

Fóllame.-Fuck me. **No me folles.** Don't fuck me.

Mámame.-Suck me. **No me mames.**Don't suck me.

Bésame.-Kiss me. **No me beses.** Don't kiss me.

Abázame.-Hug me. **No me abrace.**s Don't hug me.

Lámeme.-Rim/lick me. **No me lamas.** Don't rim/lick me.

Let's look at more commands: **You (tú)** (familiar) **You (Ud.)** (formal) **You (Uds.)** (plural) and **Let's**. Previously, we looked at *the command for someone you know well, a new buddy.* Now, let's look at the others. For the formal commands we use the *Yo* form present tense, dropping the *O* and adding some different endings. And oh, yes, there are irregular commands. Remember to make them negative place NO before the affirmative command. You'll see what I mean. **For the rest of the book, I will not underline the nature stressed vowel. Consult the pronunciation guide.** *¡Que te diviertas y gózalas!* = *Have fun and enjoy them!*

Infinitive	*comer –to eat*	
Yo	*comø*	
Tú	*come*	*eat!-you*
Ud.	*coma*	*eat!-you*
Uds.	*coman*	*eat!-all of you*
Let's	*comamos*	*Let's eat*

26

To eat -**comer**
comø
come
coma
coman
omamos

No comas   *don't eat!*
No coma
No coman
No comamos   *Let's not eat*

To help-**ayudar**

ayudø

ayuda   **help**

ayude   **help**

ayuden   **help(all of you)**

ayudemos   **Let's help**

To go-i**r**
voy

ve   **go**   **no vayas-don't go**

vaya   **go**   **no vaya-don't go**

vayan   **go**   **no vayan-don't go**

vayamos o vamos   **let's go…nos vayamos - let's not go**

To go away-**irse**
me voy
vete   **no te vayas**

váyase

váyanse

váyamonos o vámonos- no nos vayamos o no nos vamos

MORE USEFUL COMMANDS:

To hug **abrazar**
abrazø

abraza	**hug**
abrace	**hug**
abracen	**hug(all of you)**
abracemos	**Let's hug**

no abraces   *don't hug*
no abrace
no abracen
no abracemos *Let's not hug*
                I hope you get the picture about commands

To kiss-**besar**
besø

besa

bese

besen

besemos

28

Have you noticed the changes form buddy command to the formals?

To watch-**mirar**

mirø

mira   **no mires**

mire

miren

miremos

To look for-**buscar**

buscø

busca   **no busques**

busque

busquen

busquemos

To walk-**caminar**

caminø

camina   **no camines**

camine

caminen

caminemos

To pay -**pagar**
Pagø

paga   **no pagues**

pague

pague

paguemos

To play-**jugar**
juegø

juega   **no juegues**

juegue

jueguen

juguemos   **no juguemos**

To fuck-**follar**
follø

folla   **no folles**

folle

follen

follemos   **no follemos**

To fuck-**coger**
cojø

coje   **no cojas**

oja

cojan

cojamos   **no cojamos**

30

To give-**dar**

doy

da   **no des**

dé

den

demos   **no demos**

To be -**ser**

soy

sé   **no seas**

sea

sean

seamos   **no seamos**

To touch-**tocar**

tocø

toca   **no**   **toques**

toque

toquen

toquemos   **no**   **toquemos**

To suck-**mamar**

mamø

mama   **no mames**

mame

mamen

mamemos   **no mamemos**

To suck-**chupar**

chupø

chupa   **no chupes**

chape

chupen

chupemos   **no chupemos**

A few more, so you get the picture.

To let/allow-**dejar**

dejø

deja   **no dejes**

deje

dejen

dejemos   **no dejemos**

To permit-**permitir**

permitø

permite   **no permitas**

permita

permitan

permitamos   **no permitamos**

To go to bed-**acostarse**
me acuestø

acuéstate   **no te acuestes**

acuéstese

acuéstense

acostémnos   **no nos acostemoss**

To take a bath-**bañarse**
me bañø

báñate   **no te bañes**

báñese

báñense

bañémonos   **no nos bañemos**

To wash-**lavarse**
me lavø

lávate   **no te laves**

lávese

lávense

lavémonos   **no nos lave**

Now, don't get frustrated with the above commands; yes, they are very different but, I will be using them in context, so no frustrations. Ok?

*Now at a glance, let's look at some other important verbs that may be of help later in your conversation/ travel or on the World Wide Web. I will be using the **I**, **You**, **He** and **We** forms in the **PRESENT TENSE**, remembering that if you put **no** before each one, you have made it **negative**.*

To kiss-**besar**

beso	**I kiss**
besas	**you kiss**
besa	**he kisses**
besamos	**we kiss**

no beso	*I don't kiss*
no besas	*you don't kiss*
no besas	*he doesn't kiss*
no besamos	*we don't kiss*

To fuck-**coger**

cojo

coges

coge

cogemos

To fuck-follar
follo

follas

folla

follamos

To hug -**abrazar**

abrazo   I hug

abrazas   you hug

abraza   he hugs

abrazamos   we hug

To come(cum) **correrse**

me corro

te corres

se corre

nos corremos

To come- venir

vengo

vienes

viene

venimos

To come(finish)-acabar

acabo

acabas

acaba

acabamos

to speak -**hablar**

hablo	**I speak**
hablas	**you speak**
habla	**he speaks**
hablamos	**we speak**

to suck -**mamar**

mamo

mamas

mama

mamamos

To suck-chupar

chupo

chupas

chupa

chupamos

to walk-**andar**

ando

andas

anda

andamos

to look at-**mirar**

miro

miras

mira

miramos

to look for-**buscar**

busco	I look for
buscas	you look for
busca	he looks for
buscamos	we look for

to want-**querer**

quiero

quieres

quiere

queremos

to love -amar	amo	amas	ama	amamos
querer	quiero	--quieres	–quiere	-queremos
to smoke-fumar	fumo	fumas	fumas	fumamos
to put into-meter(se)	(me) meto	(te)metes		
	(se)mete	(nos)metemos		
to take out-sacar	saco	sacas	saca	sacamos
to like -gustarle	me gusta	te gusta		
	le gusta	nos gusta		
	me gustan	te gustan		
	le gustan	nos gustan		
to wish/desire-desear	--deseo	deseas	desea	deseamos
to drink-tomar	tomo	omas	toma	tomamos
beber	bebo	bebes	bebe	bebemos

	I	*You*	*He*	*We*
to swallow-tragar	trago	tragas	traga	tragamos
to chew -mascar	masco	mascas-	masca-	mascamos
to give -dar	doy	das	da	damos
to write-escribir	escribo-	escribes-	escribe-	escribimos
to go back-regresar	regreso-	regresas-	regresa-	regresamos
to make/do-hacer	hago	haces	hace	hacemos

to put/place-**poner**

pongo

pones

pone

pomemos

to be able-**poder**

puedo	I can
puedes	you can
puedes	he can
podemos	we can

to say/tell-**decir**

digo

dices

dice

decimos

to have-**tener**

tengo

tienes

tiene

tenemos

to live -**vivir**

vivo

vives

vive

vivimos

to go-**ir a**

voy   I am going

vas   you are going

va   he is going

vamos   we are going or let's go

to see   -**ver**

veo

ves

ve

vemos

to think-**pensar**

pienso   I think

piensas   you think

piensa   he thinks

pensamos   we think

40

to understand-**comprender**

comprendo

comprendes

comprende

comprendemos

to understand-**entender**

entiendo

entiende

entiende

entendemos

As you may have notice some of the above have irregular forms, don't worry about the how and why at this moment. The past tense of many Spanish verbs is irregular, and again there is not a grammar lesson needed. Just be aware of some changes. One may consult a Spanish grammar text for more explanations. *¿Está bien? Is that ok?*

Now, on to the Body parts. That's what I want to know.

Quiero saber las partes del cuerpo. = *I want to know the body parts.*

The

HUMAN BODY

and

The Essencial Parts That Attract Us To It!

El Cuerpo Humano
The Human Body

The Man's Body	**El Cuerpo del hombre.**
You have a nice body	**Tienes un buen cuerpo.**
He has a nice body	**Él tiene un buen cuerpo.**

With the body parts we use the definite article with each part. Note the gender of each body part. Afterwards we will see how to use them. *Ay, de mí. Me gusta saber eso* = *Oh, my. I like to know that*

Head	**la cabeza**
Face	**la cara**
Mouth	**la boca**
Lips	**los labios**
Tongue	**la lengua**
Nose	**la nariz**
Eyes	**los ojos**
Ears	**las orejas**
Hair	**el pelo/el cabello**
Checks	**las mejillas**
Neck	**el cuello**
Shoulders	**los hombros**
Arms	**los brazos**

Wrists	**las muñecas**
Hands	**las manos**
Fingers	**los dedos (de la mano)**
Chest	**el pecho**
Waist	**la cintura**
Legs	**las piernas**
Thighs	**los muslos**
Knees	**las rodillas**
Ankles	**los tobillos**
Feet	**los pies**
Toes	**los dedos (del pie)**
Buttocks	**las nalgas**
The face	**La Cara**
Forehead	**la frente**
Nose	**la nariz**
Eyes	**los ojos**
Eyebrows	**las cejas**
Eyes lashes	**las pestañas**
The chin	**la mandíbula**
	el mentón
Outer ears	**las orejas**
Inner ears	**los oídos**
Moustache	**el bigote**
Sideburns	**las patillas**

Beard	**la barba**
Goatee	**el candado**
The hand and arm	**la mano y el brazo**
Shoulder	**el hombro**
Arm	**el brazo**
Elbow	**el codo**
Wrist	**la muñeca**
Hand	**la mano**
Fingers	**los dedos**
Knockles	**los nudillos**
Finger nails	**las uñas**

Have you noticed singular and plural words?. A short look to see the why. OK?

el - *the* is masculine and singular and the plural is **los**, still meaning *the*.

la - *the* is feminine and singular and the plural is **las**, still meaning *the*.

*The noun is also made plural but adding **S** if it ends in a vowel, and add **ES** if it ends in consonant.*

eye	**el ojo**	eyes	**los ojos**
leg	**la pierna**	legs	**las piernas**

We also have *A* and *AN* which is **UN** and **UNA** that also has a plural. But, in the plural it changes meanings. *Miremos = Let's look.*

a finger	**un** dedo	some fingers	**unos** dedos
an ear	**una** oreja	some ears	**unas** orejas

Ok, now other important parts of the body.

The COCK/DICK and the PENIS.

cock/dick/penis	*el pene**	*un pene**
(most used terms)*	*la verga**	*una verga**
	*la polla**	*una polla**
	el palo	**un palo**
	el pito	**un pito**
	la pinga*	**una pinga***
	el rabo	**un rabo**
	la porra	**una porra**
	el cipote	**un cipote**
	el bicho	**un bicho**
	el órgano	**un órgano**
	la herramienta	**el equipo**
	el paquete o paquetote	

cocksucker/dicksucker	**un mamador**
	un mamaverga

46

un chupador

un chupapolla

big cock/dick

   una verga grande *or* *un vergón (a big dick guy)*

   una polla grande *or un pollón*

the head of the cock/dick

el capullo

la cabeza

el glande

nice cock/dick

una buena verga

una buena polla

sweet cock/dick

una verga dulce

una polla dulce

delicious cock/dick

una verga deliciosa

una polla deliciosa

long cock/dick

una verga larga

una polla larga

fat/thick cock/dick

una verga gorda

una polla gorda

A few phrases that I know you will like.

I like to suck big dicks.

Me gusta mamar vergas grandes

Me gusta mamar pollas grandes

Me gusta chupar vergas grandes

Do you like to suck?   **¿Te gusta mamar?**

                                Te gusta chupar?

Do you want to suck me off? **¿Quieres mamármela?**

                                ¿Quieres chupármela?

I want to fuck you with my big dick/cock.

Quiero follarte con mi polla grande

Quiero cogerte con mi verga grande.

Suck me.   **Mámame**

                                Chúpame

Suck me off.   **Mámamela**

                                Chúpamela

Swallow my cum!   **¡Traga mi leche!**

Swallow my hot cum!   **¡Traga mi leche caliente!**

Swallow my delicious cum!   **¡Traga mi deliciosa leche!**

Swallow it all!   **¡Trágala!**

I want it all.   **Quiero toda.**

Wow, enough for the moment with *Vergas, Pollas, Pingas y Penes*.

Let's look as the '**ASS**

Ass	el culo *	un culo*
	el culito	un
culito		
	el trasero	un
trasero		
	el hueco	un
hueco		
tight ass	**un culo apretado**	
checks/buttocks	**las nalgas**	
tight checks/ass/buttocks	**las nalgas apretadas**	
the ass hole	**el ano**	
	el ojo del culo	
	agujero	
	hoyo	
to kiss an ass	**besar el culo**	
to lick an ass	**lamer(le) el culo**	
to rim	**lamer(le) el culo**	
a rim job	**el beso negro**	

A few hot expressions: *Fantástico - Fantastic*

I want to fuck your tight ass

Quiero follar tu culo apretado

I want your sweet little ass.   **Quiero tu culito**

I want to put it in your hole.

Quiero meterla en tu agujero

I want to rim you good.   **Quiero lamerte bien**

I like your ass   **Me gusta tu culo.**

You have a nice ass.

Tienes un buen culo –Tienes un culo bueno

You have a real sweet ass

Tienes un dulce culo – Tienes un culo muy dulce

You want me to fuck your tight ass?

¿Quieres que yo te folle tu culo apretado.

Yes, I want you to fuck (my tight ass)with your big cock.
Quiero que me cojas (el culo apretado)con tu verga grande.

You want a rim job?   **¿Quieres el beso negro?**

I want a rim job.   **Sí, quiero el beso negro.**

I want your hot tongue up my ass

Quiero tu lengua caliente dentro mi culo.

Ok, let's slow down here for a moment. There are a few other things we need to know and be able to express. The A, B, C section is coming up soon. So hold tight.

GAY ..... GAY ..... GAY

A few important phrases to help you express 'gayness'. *Vamos a ver – Let's see. The term gay is known throughout the world, but there are other expressions that you need and should know.*

Are you gay?	**¿Eres gay?**
Yes, I am gay.	**Sí, soy gay.**
Is he gay?	**¿Es él gay?**
Yes, he is gay.	**Sí, él es gay.**
No, he isn't gay.	**No, no es gay.**
Are they gay?	**¿Son gay?**
Yes, they are gay.	**Sí, son gay.**
Are all of you gay?	**¿Son ustedes gay?**
Yes, we are gay.	**Sí, somos gay.**
It is obvious.	**Es obio.**
He is a……	**Él es……**
Homosexual	**homosexual**
Queer	**joto**

Sissy	**maricón**
Fag/queen	**maricón**
	marica
	mariquita
	mariposa
queen	**reina**
	loca
	pájaro
male prostitute	**puto**
hustler	**chapero**
transvestite	**travesti**
bisexual	**bisexual**
He's in the closet.	**Él está en _el closet._**

He tries to be _macho_ but he is a queer.

Él trata de ser _macho_ pero es un maricón.

He is gay for pay.	**Él es gay por pago.**

Oh, by the way, I do have a section devoted to the misconceptions and misunderstandings of _machismo._ I think that section will open your eyes to a better understanding of _MACHO._

El SEXO:

I know that this book will help you to acquire many needed expressions that are important in language usage, but I MUST EXPRESS A SERIOUS CONCERN.

PLEASE, PLEASE USE CAUTION WITH ALL SEXUAL PRACTICES HERE IN THE UNITED STATES OR ABROAD.

Remember, when you hook up with someone, BE INTELLIGENT!!! *You are not just having sex with one person but with everyone else that he has had a relation with, as well as he with yours.* PRACTICE SAFE SEX. It is a serious matter of YOUR LIFE. SEXUAL TRANSMITTED DISEASES are not worth the risk.

AIDS and STDS ARE MORE PREVELENT IN MANY OF THE DEVELOPING COUNTRIES. A GOOD PIECE OF ASS OR COCK IS NOT THE RISK OF SUICIDE!!!!!!

DEMAND AND INSIST ON USING *CONDOMS* FOR ALL SEXUAL PLESURES, *with a WATER BASED LUBRICANT.*

ABC's

English
to
Spanish

How To Express
Your Desires!

A B C's

(English to Spanish)

A Gay Man's or any Man's ABC's

In this section of the book I have underscored the natural stressed sounds to help you along but after awhile I hope you get the picture, because later I will not underscore them.

Diviértete-*Enjoy yourself.*

A

Abuse	**el ab<u>u</u>so...**
Emotional	**...emocio<u>nal</u>**
Physical	**...f<u>í</u>sico**
Sexual	**...sex<u>ual</u>**
Mental	**...men<u>tal</u>**
Psychogical	**...psico<u>ló</u>gico**
Abusive	**ab<u>u</u>so/abu<u>s</u>ivo**
He is very...	**Él es muy abu<u>s</u>ivo.**
(to) Abuse	**abu<u>s</u>ar**
Don't abuse me.	**¡No me ab<u>u</u>ses!**
Abuse me.	**Ab<u>ú</u>same**

55

I don't want him to abuse me.	**No qui_ero él me ab_use.**
I want to abuse him.	**Qui_ero abu_sarlo**
Acquaintance	**un cono_cido**
He's an….	**Él es un cono_cido**
To get to know	**Cono_cer** *(yo cono_zco)*
I don't know you.	**No te cono_zco.**
I know you.	**Te cono_zco.**
You want to know me?	**¿Qui_eres cono_cerme?**
Yes, I do…	**Sí, qui_ero cono_certe.**

I would like to know you better. **Me gusta cono_certe mej_or.**

You should get to know him better. **Debes cono_cerlo mej_or.**

Get to know me!	**¡Con_ózcame!**
I don't want to know him.	**No qui_ero cono_cerlo**

Damn, he is hot.
    I want you to introduce me to him.
Ay, ca_rajo. Él es muy cal_iente.
        Qui_ero que me pres_entes a él.
                o
        Qui_ero que me lo pres_entes.

Acquired Immune Deficiency Syndrome(AIDS)
el S_índrome de la Inmunodefic_iencia Adqui_rida- el SIDA

Does he have AIDS?	**¿T_iene el SIDA?**
No, he doesn't have AIDS.	**No, él no t_iene el SIDA.**

56

Do you have AIDS?	**¿Tienes el SIDA?**
No, I don't have AIDS	**No, no tengo el SIDA**
He has AIDS.	**Él tiene el SIDA.**
Safe sex.	**El sexo seguro.**

(In many developing countries **el SIDA** is very prevalent. *Don't risk your life! Live is worth living.* Amigos. **ALWAYS PRACTICE SAFE SEX.)**

¡USE CONDÓN!

(to) Adore	**adorar**
I adore you.	**Te adoro.**
Do you adore him?	**¿Lo adoras?**
I adore him a lot.	**Lo adoro mucho.**
I adore you a lot.	**Te adoro mucho.**
We adore you .	**Te adoramos.**
We adore each other.	**Nos adoramos mucho.**
Do you adore me?	**¿ Me adoras?**
Of course, I adore you.	**Sí, cómo no. Te adoro mucho.**

Adult	**un adulto**
Adventure	**una aventura**

I want an adventure with you .

Quiero una aventura contigo.

Do you want a sexual adventure?

¿Quieres una aventura sexual?

Sure, a sexual adventure in the jungle.

Seguro, una aventura en *la selva*.

Oh, baby. Let's go! **¡Vamos nene!**

Adventurer **un aventurero** I am an adventurer.

Are you? **Soy aventurero. ¿Eres tú?**

Affection **el cariño, el afecto**

Affectionate **cariñoso/ afectuoso**

He is very affectionate. **Él es muy cariñoso.**

Are you affectionate? **¿Eres cariñoso?**

Yes, I am very affectionate. **Sí, soy muy cariñoso.**

Amorous/loving **amoroso**

He is so loving. **Él es tan amoroso.**

He is not very loving. **Él no es muy amoroso.**

Anal **anal/ano**

Anal sex **el sexo anal**

Sodomy **la sodamía**

I like anal sex. **Me gusta sexo anal.**

¿Do you like anal sex? **¿Te gusta sexo anal?**

Aphrodisiac **afrodesíaco**

58

(to) Arouse/excite	**excitar/provocar**
Arouse me	**¡Excítame!**
	¡Provócame!
Don't excite me.	**¡No me excites!**
	¡No me provoques!
I want to arouse you.	**Deseo exitarte.**
I am going to excite you.	**Voy a exitarte.**
Ass	**(el) culo**
Tight…	**…apretado**
Cute…	**…chulo**
Hot…	**…caliente**
Sexy…	**…sexy**
A piece of …	**Un cacho de carne.**
	Un pedazo de carne.

I want your tight ass.

Quiero tu culo apretado.

..to get a hot piece of ass

Agarrar un culo caliente.

Conseguir un culo caliente.

el culo/la carne (la carne-meat … may also be cock/dick)

I got a hot piece of ass.

Agarro un cacho de carne caliente.

Consigo un pedazo de carne caliente.

I would like to get some nice ass.

Me gustaría agarrar un buen culo.

I've got the ass you want.

Tengo el culo que quieres.

I want your tail baby.

Quiero tus nalgas, nene.

He has a nice ass.

Él tiene buenas nalgas.

You have a really *nice ass*.

Tienes nalgas *muy buenas*.

….. nice and round

……………*buenas y redondas*.

…..a bouble ass.-**Un culo borbujado.**

…..to fuck the ass   **Follar el culo.**

                                             Coger el culo.

I want to fuck your ass   **Quiero**

follarte/cogerte en el culo.

I want to fuck you in the mouth.

Quiero follarte/cogerte en la boca.

Fuck me in the ass.

¡Fóllame/cójeme en el culo!

Fuck me in the mouth.

¡Fóllame/cójeme en la boca!

Asshole   **el ano/el ojo/el culero/el hoyo**

I want to put my cock in your asshole.

Quiero meter la verga en tu ano

Quiero meter la polla en tu culo.

I want to put it in you.

Quiero metértela.

I want to fuck you in your hole.

Quiero follarte/cojerte en *tu hoyo*.

..one who takes it in the ass..

…un culero

..tight ass   **…culo apretado**

                 …culo prieto

                 …nalgas prietas

                 …nalgas apretadas

You have a tight ass.

Tienes nalgas prietas

Tienes culo prieto

I like a nice tight ass to fuck.

Me gusta un culo apretado para coger/follar.

B

Babe/baby	**Nene**
	Baby
	Muñeco(doll baby)
	Papi(daddy)
Balls	**los huevos**
	los cojones
	las bolas
	las pelotas

I want to suck your balls.

    Quiero chupar tus huevos.

I like big balls.	**Me gustan bolas grandes.**
I like hairless balls.	**Me gustan pelotas sin vellos**

I like hairy balls.---**Me gustan pelotas con muchos vellos.**

I like sucking your balls.----**Me gustan mamar tus huevos.**

You have sweet balls baby	**Tienes huevos dulces, nene.**
Suck my balls.	**Mama mis huevos.**
scrotum	**el escroto**
Bareback	**sin condón**
	a pelo
	a lo bruto

I want to fuck you bareback.

uiero cogerte sin condón.

> Fuck me bareback.

> **Cójeme a lo bruto.**

Do you like to fuck bareback?

¿Te gusta follar a palo?

> Fuck me bareback.

> **Fóllame a los bruto.**

| package | **el paquete** |
| big package | **el paquetote** |

> You have a nice package.

> **Tienes buen paquetote.**

> I like the package I see.

> **Me gusta el paquete que veo.**

> …. a delicious package….**un paquete delicioso.**

| Bear | **el oso** |
| Bears | **los osos** |

| Little bear/cub | **el osito/los ositos** |
| (to) Beat | **golpear/pegar** |

| …beat me | **¡Golpéame!** |
| …don't' beat me | **No me golpees** |

(to) Beat your meat	**manojársela**
	jalársela
	puñeteársela
	chaqueteársela

I like to jerk off.	**Me gusta jalármela.**
I have to beat off.	**Tengo que manojármela.**
Do you like to beat off?	**¿Te gusta jalártela?**

I jack off with two hands.

Me la chaqueteo con dos manos.

He jacks off three times a day.

Él se la jala tres veces al día.

We beat of together.

Nos la manojamos juntos.

Do you jerk off often?

¿Te la puñeteas a menudo?

| Jack me off, baby. | **¡Jálamela! Nene/Baby.** |
| Bed | **la cama** |

| Let's go to bed. | **Vamos a la cama.** |
| …from bed to bed. | **…de cama en cama** |

…he goes from bed to bed.

Él va de cama en cama.

| (to go to) Bed | **acostarse(ue)** |

I want to go to bed with you.

Quiero acostarme contigo.

Do you want to go to bed with me?

¿Quieres acostarte conmigo?

Go to bed with me!

¡Acuéstate conmigo!

Don't go to bed with him!

No te acuestes con él.

Let's go to bed.

Vamos a acostarnos

¡Acostémonos!

Let's not go to bed.

No vamos a acostarnos.

No nos vamos a acostar.

¡No nos acostemos!

He wants to go to bed with me.

Él quiere acostarse contigo

Let's go to bed.

Vamos a la cama.

You want to go to bed, daddy?

¿Quieres ir a la cama, Papi?

I would like to fuck in bed.

Deseo follarte en la cama.

I should/ought to fuck in the bed.

Debo cogerte en la cama.

You want to fuck in the bed.

¿Deseas cogerme en la cama?

I want to fuck you any place.

Quiero follarte en cualquier lugar.

You know I want to go to bed with you .

Sabes que quiero acostarme contigo.

You know I want to go to be with you.

Sabes que deseo ir a la cama contigo.

Bi-sexual   **bisexual**

Bi-sexuality   **bisexualidad**

He's not gay but bisexual

Él no es gay sino bisexual.

I'm not into bisexuals.

No tengo interés en los bisexuales.

I want a gay man.

Deseo un hombre gay.

I cannot share a man with a woman.

No puedo compartir un hombre con una mujer.

He cannot be both.

Él no puede ser ambos dos.

(to) Bite   **morder(ue)**

     Bite my nipples.   **¡Muerde los pezones!**

     I like to bite nipples.

Me gusta morder los pezones.

     I want to suck your nipples.

Quiero chupar tus pezones.

     I love to suck on your nipples.

Quiero mamar tus pezones.

     Suck my nipples!   **¡Chupa mis pezones!**

     passion mark   **un chupetón**

     He has a hicky on his neck.

Él tiene un chupetón en el cuello.

     I like passion marks hidden.

Me gustan chupetones escondidos.

     Put a passion mark close to my cock.

Pon un chupetón cerca de mi verga (mi polla).

Blow Job   **una mamada.**

     Give me a blowjob!   **¡Dame una mamada!**

     I like BJ's.   **Me gustan mamadas.**

     He gives good BJ's.

Él da buenas mamadas.

He's a good cocksucker.

Él es un buen mamador. (mamador bueno)

I'm a good cocksucker.

Soy buen mamador

Can I give you a blowjob?

¿Puedo darte una mamada?

Oh, yea. Suck me. I like blowjobs.

Sí, mámame. Me gustan mamadas.

I want a blowjob.

Deseo una mamada.

Quiero una mamada.

I want a good blowjob.

Quiero una buena mamada.

Bondage   **la esclavitud**

I don't like bondage.

No me gusta la esclavidad.

I need a slave boy.

Necesito un niño esclavo.

¿You want to be my slave boy?

¿Deseas ser mi esclavo?

Yes, I want to be your slave boy.

Sí, Quiero ser tu esclavo.

Come here slave. Suck me off!

Ven acá esclavo. Mámamela

Boy	**chico**
	muchacho
	niño
…boy toy	**un juguete**
…party boy	**un parrandero**
…boyfriend	**novio**
	amante (lover)
	amigo

I want a boy to fuck.

Quiero un muchacho para coger.

I need a boy toy.	**Necesito un juguete.**
You want a boy toy?	**¿Quieres un juguete?**

We want a party boy.

Queremos un parrandero

He is my boyfriend.	**Él es mi novio.**
We are boyfriends.	**Somos novios**
We are lovers.	**Somos amantes**
Where are the boys?	**¿Dónde están los chicos?**

Breeders	**los procreadores**	**los creadores**

Buddy	**amigo íntimo**

He's my butt buddy   **Él es mi amigo íntimo.**

He's my fuck buddy.   **Él es mi amigo íntimo.**

… We fuck every day.

Cojemos todos los días.

Follamos todos los días.

Bulge   **el paquete**

                    el regalo

He shows a nice bulge.

Él muestra un buen paquete.

He's got a big bulge.

Él tiene paquete grande.

Man. What a big package!

Hombre. ¡Qué paquetote!

He is showing a huge package.

Él marca un paquete gigante.

I want what's in his pants.

Quiero lo que tiene en los pantalones.

Butch   **macho**

He is real butch.   **Él es muy macho.**

He thinks he is butch.   **Él piensa que es macho.**

…his legs spread wide open

…sus piernas abre a los cielos.

…and he sucks big cocks.

…y mama pollas grandes. (vergas grandes).

He is physically macho.

Él es macho físicamente.

…but he is a real lady/queen. …

pero es muy maricón (puto)

Butt/Buttocks   **las nalgas**

  butt plug   **un tapón para el culo**

He has a nice ass.

Él tiene buenas nalgas.

I like his sweet ass.

Me gustan las buenas nalgas.

I want to fuck his ass.

Quiero follar(coger) las nalgas.

You like my ass?

¿Te gustan las nalgas?

Oh, baby. I want your ass.

Oh, nene. Quiero tus nalgas.

C

(to) Caress/Cuddle/Squeeze   **acariciar**

    I want to squeeze your balls.

Quiero acariciar tus huevos.

    Do you like to cuddle?

¿Te gusta acariciar?

    I would like to caress you .

Me gustaría acariciarte.

    You want to cuddle?

¿Deseas acariciar?

    Caress me/ Hug me.   **Acaríciame.**

Carnal   **carnal**

Celibate   **célibe**

    To be celibate.   **ser célibe.**

    I am celibate.   **Soy célibe.**

    I have been celibate for 2 years.

    Hace 2 años que soy célibe.

    He sido célibe por 2 años.

    I am not celibate.   **No soy célibe.**

Celibacy   **el celibato**

    I practice celibacy.   **Practico el celibato.**

    He doesn't practice… **Él no practica el celibato.**

(to)Charm/really like   **encantarle (a)**

You charm me a lot.	**Me encantas mucho.**
I really like you.	**Me encantas mucho.**
a Charm/spell	**un encanto**
He has a loving charm.	**Él tiene un encanto**

amoroso.

You are a charmer.	**Eres un encantador**
(to)Cheat/Deceive	**engañar (a)**
Don't cheat on me.	**No me engañes.**

I don't guys who cheat.

No me gustan chicos que me engañan.

I will never cheat on you.	**No te engaño nunca.**
You are cheating on me,	**Estás engañándome,**
…and I don't like it.	**…y no me gusta**
Are you cheating on me?	**¿Me engañas?**

No baby/daddy. I would never cheat/deceive you.

Ay, no Papi, Nunca te engaño.

You are a liar.	**Eres mentiroso.**

(to) Cheat	**ponerle a cuernos.**
He is cheating.	**Le pone a cuernos.**
He is cheating on me.	**Se me pone a cuernos.**
He cheated on me.	**Se me puso a cuernos.**
Don't cheat on me.	

¡No me pongas a cuernos!

73

Cheater/Deceiver	un engañador
He's a big cheater.	

Él es un gran engañador.

I don't like cheaters.

No me gustan engañadores.

Climax/orgasm/to cum	un climax
	un orgasmo
	correrse/venir/acabar
I'm having an orgasm.	Tengo un orgasmo.
	Tengo climax
Did you cum?	¿Te corriste?
	¿Acabaste?
	¿Viniste?
I came much/a lot.	Me corrí mucho.
	Vine mucho.
	Acabé mucho.

Oh, daddy. I am cumming.

Oh, papi. estoy viniendo.

Oh, baby. Me estoy corriendo.

I want a hot orgasm with you .

Quiero orgasmo caliente contigo.

My cum is so sweet baby.

Mi leche es muy dulce, Papi.

I can cum many times for you baby.

Puedo acabar mucho para ti Papi.

(to) Copulate **copular (con)**

    Do you want to copulate? **¿Quieres copular?**

    Let's copulate! **Copulemos (Vamos a copular)**

Condom **un condón**

    Rubber **una goma**

    I need a condom. **Necesito un condón.**

Condom (cont.)

    I need a condom.

Me falta condón/preservativo.

    I won't fuck you without a condom.

No te cojo sin condón/preservativo.

No te follo sin goma.

    Fuck me with a condom.

    Cójeme con condón.

    Fóllame con condón.

    Put a condom on.

    Ponte un condón.

For safety, I will suck you, if you wear a condom.

Por seguridad, te la mamo si usas condón.

He doesn't use a protection.

Él no usa protección.

I always use protection.

Siempre uso protección.

I don't want diseases.

No quiero enfermedades.

Couple/partner   **pareja**

     Do you have a partner?   **¿Tienes pareja?**

     Do you have a boyfriend?   **¿Tienes novio?**

     No, I am single.   **No, soy soltero.**

     He has a partner. Be careful.   **Él tiene pareja.**

Cuidado.

Cross dresser   **travesti**

     I am a cross dresser.   **Soy travesti.**

     I don't like cross dressers   **No   me   gustan**

travesties.

     He wears women's clothes.

     Él usa (lleva) ropa de mujer.

(to) Cruise   **ligar (con)**

               trabajarse (a la calle) (to work the street)

     Let's go crusing the bars.

Vamos a ligar por los bares.

Let's go crusing the streets.

Vamos a ligar por las calles.

Vamos a trabajarnos a las calles

Let's work the streets.

Trabajémonos a las calles

Are you crusing me?

¿Me estás ligando conmigo?

¿Me te trabajas a mí?

Yes, I am crusing you.   **Sí, Ligo contigo.**

Sí, Te me trabajo a ti.

Why are you looking at me?   **¿Por qué me miras?**

Por qué me estás mirando?

I am looking at you because you are handsome.

Te miro porque eres muy guapo.

You are handsome too.

Eres guapo. También

(to) Cuddle with   **acurrucarse (con)**

I would like to cuddle with you .

Me gustaría acurrucarme contigo.

I want to cuddle with you .

Quiero acurracarme contigo.

Cuddle with me.

Acurrúcate conmigo.

Cuddler	**un acurracador**
I like a cuddler.	**Me gusta un acurracador.**
Are you a cuddler?	**¿Eres un acurracador?**
Yes, I am a cuddler.	**Sí, soy acurracador.**
Circumcised/Cut	**circuncidado**
	cortado
¿Are you circumcised?	**¿Eres circuncidado?**
¿Are you cut?	**¿Eres cortado?**

I like men who are cut.

Me gustan hombres cortados.

Me gustan hombres circuncidado.

He's not circumcised. **Él no es circuncidado.**

Él no es cortado.

Most Latinos are not circumcised.

Mucho latinos no son circuncidados.

D

Date	**una cita/un compromiso**

I have a date tonight with a handsome guy.

Tengo una cita con un hombre guapo

Tengo un compromiso con un hombre guapo.

Do you have a date?   **¿Tienes cita?**

¿Tienes compromiso?

We have a date.

Tenemos cita.

Tenemos compromiso.

I have a date with an angel.

Tengo una cita con un ángel.

Dildo   **consolador/dildo**

He likes to use a dildo.

A él le gusta usar un consolador.

He like big dildos.

A él le gustan consoladores grandes.

A él le gustan dildos grandes.

We use a dildo to enrich our sex.

Usamos consolador para enriquecer nuestro sexo.

Ultilizamos dildo para enriquecer nuestro sexo.

He uses a big dildo every night.

Él usa un dildo grande todas las noches.

Él usa un consolador grande cada noche.

Where can I buy a dildo?

¿Dónde puedo comprar un consolador?

They sell them en sex shops.

Se venden en tiendas de sexo.

Let's go get(buy) one.

Vamos a comprar uno.

…a big one.   **…un grande.**

I need a dildo tonight.

Necesito un consolador.

I want a big dildo.

Quiero un consolador grande.

Dirty   **sucio**

A dirty joke.   **Un chiste verde.**

A dirty mind.   **Un pervertido.**

A dirty of man.   **Un Viejo verde.**

He is so dirty that he needs a bath.

Él está tan sucio y necesita bañarse

I am dirty. I need a shower.

Estoy sucio. Necesito un baño. (una ducha).

Doggie style   **a cuatro patas**

I want to fuck you doggy style.

Quiero follarte a cuatro patas.

Quiero cogerte a cuatro patas.

He fuck me doggy style.   **Me cogió a cuatro patas.**

Do you like doggy style.   **¿Te gusta coger a cuatro patas?**

Fuck me doggy style.   **Fóllame a cuatro patas.**

Cójeme a cuatro patas.

Drag Queen   **una reina/ un travesti**

I like drag shows.   **Me gustan los shows de travesties**

I don't like drag shows.

No me gustan espectáculos de travesties.

There is a drag show tonite.   **Hay un show esta noche.**

Let's go to the drag show.   **Vamos al show.**

Drop   **una gota**

...a drop of cum   **..una gota de leche.**

I want every drop of your delicious cum.

Quiero cada gota de tu deliciosa leche.

Do you swallow?

¿Tragas?

I will swallow every drop of your cum.

Trago cada gota de tu leche.

I like to swallow it.   **Me gusta tragarla.**

Let me swallow it.   **Déjame tragarla.**

Don't waste a drop.   **No pierdas ninguna gota.**

E

(to) Ejaculate   **eyacular**

Ejaculation	la eyaculación
...premature	...precoz
(to) Embrace/hug	abrazar (a)

I really want to hug you.
Tengo muchas ganas de abrazarte.
Please, hug me.
Por favor, abrázame
Don't hug me in public.
No me abraces en público.

Let's hug each other. I don't care.
Abracémonos. No me importa.

an Embrace/hug	**un abrazo**
a strong hug	**un fuerte abrazo**
a big hug	**un abrazote**
many hugs	**muchos abrazos**
many hugs and kisses	**muchos abrazos y besos**
hugs and kisses	**abrazos y besos**

strong hugs and tender kisses

fuertes abrazos y tiernos besos (abrazos fuertes y besos tiernos)

Do you need a hug?	**¿Necesitas un abrazo?**

Yes, I need a big hug.

Sí, necesito un fuerte abrazo.

I am going to hug you .   **Voy a abrazarte**

Every body needs a hug   **Todo el mundo**

necesita un abrazo.

Everyone need a hug and kiss.

Todo el mundo necesita abrazo y beso.

(to) Enjoy/Have fun   **gozar (de)**

divertirse

pasarla bien

I want to enjoy you.   **Quiero gozarte.**

I want to enjoy every delicious inch.

Quiero gozarte de cada delicioso centímetro.

Quiero gozarte de cada deliciosa pulgada.

What do you enjoy more?   **¿Qué gozas más?**

I enjoy you fucking me.   **Te gozo follándome.**

Te gozo cogiéndome.

I enjoy sucking your off.   **Gozo chupándotela**

Gozo mamándotela

Enjoy it!   **¡Gózala!**

I hope you enjoyed it!   **Espero que la gozaste.**

Did you enjoy it?   **¿La Gozaste?**

Yes, I enjoyed it a lot.   **Sí, la gocé mucho**

Erect/hard	duro/a
	erecto/a
	tieso/a
a hard cock	una verga dura un pene
duro	
	una polla tiesa
	una pinga erecta
Do you have a hard cock?	¿Tienes verga dura?
	¿Tienes polla tiesa?
Is your cock hard?	¿Está dura?
Are you hard?	¿Estás dura?
I am hard.	Estoy dura.
I was hard.	Estaba tiesa

You like a my nice hard cock up your ass?

¿Te gusta mi verga dura dentro tu culo?

Oh, Yes, I want your hard cock deep in my ass.

Oh, Sí, quiero tu verga dura al fondo de mi culo.

It was hard. I don't know what happened.

Estaba dura y no sé lo que pasó.

Get it hard again.

Ponte dura otra vez.

Suck it and it'll get hard again.

Mámamela y se pone(se pondrá) dura de nuevo.

Get it had!	**¡Ten dura!**
Erotic	**erótico**
Eroticism	**eroticísmo**
Exotic	**exótico**

I had an erotic dream about you.

Tuve un sueño erótico de ti.

I want to go to an exotic place with you.

Deseo ir a un lugar exótico contigo.

Let's go to an exotic place. Just you and I.

Vamos a un lugar exótico. Sólo Tú y yo.

You are really erotic and you excite me.

Eres bien erótico y me excitas mucho.

Eroticism stimulates me a lot.

El erotisísmo me estimula mucho.

It excites me. Does it you?

Me excita. ¿Y a ti, te excita?

Yes, it does a lot.

Sí, me excita mucho.

Sí, me provaca mucho.

F

Fantasy	**fantasia o sueño**

...erotic fantasy	**una fantasía erótica**
	un sueño erótico
...wet dream	**un sueño mojado**
	una fantasía mojada
...a sexual fantasy	**una fantasía sexual**
	un sueño sexual

| I dream about you. | **Sueño contigo.** |
| Do you dream about me? | **¿Sueñas conmigo?** |

I imagine that we are loving each other.

Me imagino de que estemos amándonos.

I fantasize you are hugging and kissing me.

Me imagino de me estés abrazando y besando.

Fantasize with me!

¡Imagínate conmigo!

Let's have a sexual fantasy!

¡Tengamos una fantasía sexual!

Do you have a sexual fantasy?

¿Tienes una fantasía sexual?

Yes, that we wake up in each other arms.

Sí, que nos desperemos envueltos en nuestros brazos.

Let's make our fantasies happen.

Vamos a realizar nuestras fantasías.(nuestros sueños)

(to) Feel up /grope   **toquetear**

                            manosear

That goodlooking guy felt me up.

Ese guapo me toqueteó

It felt good.   **Me sintió bien.**

When did he feel you up?   **¿Cuándo te manoseó?**

When I returned from the bathroom.

Cuando regresé del baño.

Hey, did you fell me up?

Oiga, o Oye ¿me toqueteaste?

Yes, I did. I want to get to know you.

Sí, te toqueteé. Quiero conocerte.

Why not introduce yourself?

¿Por qué no me presentaste?

I don't like being groped.

No me gusta estar toqueteado.

Please, don't touch me!

Por favor, no me toques.

Fellatio   **la felación**

Do you like fellatio?   **¿Te gusta la felación?**

Of course, I love it.   **Por supuesto, Me encanta.**

I would like to suck your cock.

Me gustaría mamártela.

Fellatio is my specialty.   **La felación es mi especialidad.**

Femme   **una pluma**

                  afeminado

Don't be femme.   **No seas una pluma.**

Not femme, please.   **Sin plumas. Por favo**

He is to femme for me.   **Él es tan afeminado para mí.**

Fetish/Kinky   **morbo**

                  fetiche

                  morboso

Do you have any fetishes?   **¿Tienes fetiches?**

Yes, I love jock straps.   **Sí, me encantan sorportes,**

I like to smell them.   **Me gusta olerlos.**

Any more?   **¿Más?**

Are you kinky?   **¿Eres morboso?**

Of course, I love being tied up on the bed.

Sí, cómo no. Me gusta estar atado en la cama.

Yes, tie me up and blind fold me.

Sí, átame y ponme bendado.

Then, suck me and pound (fuck) me.

Entonces, mámame y clávame.

Use dildos too.

Usa (Utiliza) consoladores también.

Man, you are really kinky.

Hombre, eres muy morboso.

I don't like pain. You know.

No me gusta dolor (pena). Sabes.

Flamer   **una loca**

                                 una reina

What a flamer!   **¡Qué loca!**

                                   ¡Qué reina!

I really don't like flamers

Personalmente, no me gustan las locas (las reinas).

Flasher/exhibitionist   **exhibicionista**

What an exhibitionist!   **Wow, ¡Qué exhibicionista!**

He's an exhibitionist.   **Él es exhibicionista.**

(to) Flash/show   **mostrarse(ue)**

                            exhibirse

He is flashing me.   **Se me exhibe.**

                            Se me muestra.

He like to show himself in the bathroom.

A él le gusta mostrarse en el baño.

He shows himself to every guy.

Se muestra enfrente de todos.

He has a lot to show.

Tiene mucho para mostrarse/exhibirse.

Do you like to show your cock to every guy?

¿Te gusta mostrártela a todos los hombres.

No, I only like to show it to you.

Sólo me gusta mostrámela a ti.

(to) Flatter	**echar flores**
	dar piropos
	halagar

(to) Flatter(cont.)

    My love you always flatter me.

    Mi amor, siempre me halagas.

    Mi amor, siempre me da piropos

You always flatter me.	**Siempre me echas flores.**
I like to flatter you.	**Me gusta echar flores.**
Don't flatter me!	**¡No me des piropos!**

I am not flattering you. All I say is true.

No te echo flores. Todo te digo es verdad.

…Flattery	**los piropos**
	los halagos
Flesh/meat	**la carne (cock/dick)**

    I would like to suck your flesh.

    Me gustaría mamar tu carne.

| I want your meat . | **Quiero tu carne.** |
| Your meat is delicious. | **Tu carne es deliciosa.** |

Would you like me to fuck you with my big piece of meat?

¿Te gustaría que yo te follara con mi polla grande?

¿Te gustaría que yo te cogiera con mi verga grande?

I like big pieces of meat like your hot cock.

Me gustan pedazos grandes de carne como tu pinga caliente.

~ (to) Flirt   **coquetear**

                           flirtear

Why are you flirting?

¿Por qué estás coqueteando?

I am only flirting with you .

Sólo estoy coqueteando contigo.

Don't flirt so much with other guys.

No coquetees tanto con otros hombres.

It's only flirting. Nothing serious.

Sólo flirteo, nada en serio.

Because, you know I love only you.

Porque sabes que sólo te quiero.

Are you flirting with me again?

¿Me coqueteas de nuevo?

You are a big flirt.   **Eres un gran coqueteo.**

You know I like to flirt.

Sabes que me gusta coquetear/flirtear.

Foreskin   **el precucio**

    Do you like guys with foreskin?

    ¿Te gustan hombres con precucio?

        Yes, most Latino men have foreskin.

        Sí, Muchos latinos tienen precucio.

…to pull back the foreskin   **descapullar**

Man, when he pulls back his foreskin, his big head is hot.

Hombre, cuando descapulla su cabeza grande es muy caliente.

    Pull back your foreskin   **¡Descapulla!**

Fornicate   **fornicar**

(to) have Fun   **divertirse**

           gozar (de)

           pasarla bien

Are you having a good time?	¿Te diviertes?
	¿La pasas bien?
I have a good time with you .	Me divierto mucho contigo.
	La paso bien contigo.
	Gozo mucho de ti.
It's fun.	Es divertido
You are fun baby.	Eres divertido. Papi.
Enjoy it!	¡Diviértete!
I want you to enjoy it a lot.	Deseo que te diviertas mucho.
	Deseo que la pases bien.

I always have a good time with you.

Siempre me divierto mucho contigo.

(to) Fuck	*coger
	*follar
	tirar
	ponchar
	pisar
	culear
	chichar
	clavar
	chingar(explicative explained later)
	joder(explicative explained later)

Do you want to fuck me?

¿Quieres cogerme?

¿Quieres follarme?

¿Quieres clavarme?

I really want to fuck you hard.

Quiero cogerte fuerte.

I want to fuck you doggy sytle.

Quiero clavarte a cuatro patas.

Spread your legs and let me fuck you.

Abre las piernas y déjame cogerte.

I would like to penetrate your sweet ass.

Quisiera penetrarte tu culito.

I want to put it in you deep.

Quiero metértela al fondo.

Fuck me hard. Baby.

¡Clávame fuerte! Papi.

Fill me your hot cum.

¡Llename con tu caliente leche(leche caliente)!

Let's fuck and fuck.

¡Cojamos y cojamos!

¡Follemos y follemos!

Let's fuck each other all night.

¡Cojámonos toda la noche!

Fuck me with your big dick.

¡Fóllame con tu verga grande!

Fuck me really hard.

¡   **Fóllame muy fuerte!**

I love a good fuck.

Amo una buena cogida/follada

(to) Fuck-explicative   **chingar**

                              joder

Note: Becareful with usage, they can be fighting words, specially using it with **'madre'**. Don't direct them to anyone, for your own well being. Smiles!

fucker   *chingada*

son of a fucking bitch   *hijo de la chingada*

daugther of a fuckng bitch   *hija de la chingada*

go fuck your mother   *chinga a tu madre*

(to) Fuck-explicative(cont.)   **chingar**

                              joder

Note: Becare with usage, they can be fighting words, specially using it with **'madre'**. Don't direct them to anyone, for your own well being.

go fuck/go to hell	vete a la chingada
your fucking mother	a la chingada madre

your mother's fucking cunt.
a la concha de la chingada madre

your mother's cunt	la concha de tu madre
your grandmother's cunt	la concha de tu abuela
don't fuck with me	no me chingues

you are a fucking son of a bitch.
Eres hijo de la chingada madre.

he's a fucking son of a bitch
Él es un hijo de la chingada madre.

no fucking way	a la chingada
they fucked me over	me chingaron
no fucking way	no chingues
don't fuck with me	no me mames
don't fuck with me.	no me jodas
fuck!	¡joder!

fuck you	*jódate*
fuck you!	***Chíngate***
Why are you fucking with me?	***¿Por qué me jodes?***
	¿Por qué me chingas?
Man, I fucked up.	***Hombre, Me jodí***
Are you fucking up?	***¿Estás jodiendo?***
Are you fucked up?	***¿Estás jodido?***
Did you fuck up?	***¿Jodiste?***
Man, I am fucked up.	***Hombre. Estoy jodido.***
I am going to fuck around.	***Voy a joder por ahí***
Let's go fucking around.	***Vamos a joder por ahí.***

G

(to) Gang bang	**coger en grupo**
	follar en grupo
	una colectiva
Gay	**gay**
Gay bar	**un bar gay**
...gay dance club	**...un disco gay**

…gay pride	…orgullo gay
…gay guide	…una guía gay
…gay book	…libro gay
…gay magazine	…revista gay
…gay pictures	…fotos gay
…neighborhood	…barrio gay
	…vencedario gay
… rights	…los derechos gay
…human rights	…los derechos humanos
…gay scene	…el ambiente gay
…newspaper	…el periódico gay
…gay zone	…la zona gay

Genitals	los órganos
	los genitales
(to) Get it up/get it hard	ponerse dura
	ponerse tiesa
I can't get it hard.	No puedo ponerme tiesa.
	No puedo ponerme dura
Get it hard baby.	Ponte tiesa. Nene.
Get it up.	Ponte dura.

He gets hard all the time.

Él se pone dura todo el tiempo.

He got so hard.　　　　　Él se pone tan dura.

I like a nice hard cock.

Me gusta una verga muy dura.

Let me fuck you with my hard dick.

Déjame follarte con mi polla dura.

Fuck me with your big hard dick.

¡Cójame con tu vergón bien duro!

Your big cock is good and hard.

Tu pollón está bien duro.

Oh, baby. You are nice and hard.

Oh, Papi. Estás bien dura.

Groin　　　　　　　　la ingle

Group sex/orgy　　　una orgía

Let's have an orgy!　　　　¡Tengamos una orgía!

There's an orgy at Carlos's house.

Hay una orgía en casa de Carlos.

I like orgies.　　　　　　Me gustan orgías

(to) Go down on	**chupar**
	mamar

I want to go down on you.

Quiero mamártela.

You want o go down on him?

¿Quieres mamársela?

Let's go down on him.	**¡Chupémosela!**
	Vamos a chupársela.
Go down on me.	**¡Mámamela!**
	¡Chúpamela!

Go down on us.	**¡Mámanosla!**
	¡Chúpanosla!
Go down on that big dick.	**¡Mama ese vergón!**
	¡Chupa ese pollón!
You wan to down on me?	**¿Quieres mamármela?**

(to)Go in and out	**entrar y salir**
	penetrar

My cock was going in and out real hard.

Mi verga entraba y salía muy fuerte.

Put it in slowly and take it out slowly.

¡Métemela despacio y sácamela despacio!

Put it in slowly then really fuck me hard and don't take it out.

¡Métemela despacio y entonces fóllame fuerte y no te la saques!

He goes in and out with his delicious cock.

Él entra y sale la deliciosa verga con mucha fuerza.

Put it in and don't take it out.   **¡Éntrame y no salgas!**

H

Hairy	**velludo**
	peludo
...pubic hair	**...vellos púbicos**

...pendejo(related to pubic and anal hair)

...I like hairy men   **...Me gustan hombre velludos/pelados.**

...I like a hairy cock.   **...Me gusta una verga velluda.**

...Me gusta una polla peluda.

...He has a hairy ass.   **...Él tiene el culo velludo.**

...I like a hairy chest.   **Me gusta el pecho peludo.**

...Are you hairy?   **¿Estás velludo/peludo?**

...I have hairy legs.   **Tengo vellos en las piernas.**

...I have a hairy chest.   **Tengo vellos en el pecho**

Tengo un pecho velludo.

Handjob	**una paja**
	un manojo
	un pajero
You want a handjob?	**¿Quieres un manojo?**
I will give you a handjob.	**Voy a darte una paja.**
Give me a handjob.	**¡Dame un manojo!**
(to) Masturbate/beat off/etc.	**chaquetearse**
	hacerse una paja
	jalársela
	pajearse
	masturbarse
Jack me off.	**¡chaquetéamela!**
	¡hazme una paja!
	¡jalámela!
	¡pajéamela!

Let me give you a handjob.

Permíteme hacerte una paja.

Déjame darte un manojo.

Would you like to be beat off?

¿Te gustaría pajearte?

Do you like to jackoff?	¿Te gusta jalártela?
	¿Te gusta chaquetártela?
Handcuffs	las esposas
(to) handcuff	poner las esposas
Do you have handcuffs?	¿Tienes las esposas?
I have the handcuffs.	Tengo las esposas.
Put on the handcuffs.	¡Ponme las esposas!
Don't handcuff me.	
¡No me pongas las esposas!	
Handcuff me to the bed.	
¡Ponme las esposas en la cama!	

Take off the handcuffs.

¡Saca las esposas!

I don't like handcuffs.

No me gustan las esposas.

Hard	dura
	tiesa
(to) to get it Hard	ponerse tiesa
	ponerse dura
(to) have a Hard cock.	tener polla dura
	tener verga dura
	tener pinga tiesa

I have a hard on.	**Tengo polla dura.**
	Tengo verga dura.
I'm hard.	**Estoy dura.**
	Estoy tiesa.
Are you hard?	**¿Estás dura?**
Were you hard?	**¿Estabas tiesa?**
(to) give Head	**dar una mamada**
	chupar
	mamar
I want to give you head.	**Quiero darte una mamada.**
Give me head.	**¡Dame una mamada!**
I like blowjobs.	**Me gustan mamadas.**

(to) Give Head(cont.)

We give good head. **Damos buenas mamadas.**

The best head/blowjobs. **Las mejores mamadas.**

He really knows how to give good head.

Él sabe dar buenas mamadas.

I know how to give good head/blowjobs.

Yo sé dar buenas mamadas.

Hickey/passion mark	**un chupetón**
	un mordisco

HIV	el SIDA
…positive	…positivo
…negative	…negativo
…virus	…virus
…positive	…seropositivo
…negative	…seronegativo

I am negative.	**Soy negativo.**
I am positive.	**Soy positivo.**
I have the virus.	**Tengo el virus.**
I don't have AIDS.	**No tengo el SIDA.**
I am HIV positive.	**Soy positivo.**
He is negative.	**Él es negativo**
We are negative.	**Somos negativos.**

I have been tested and I am negative.

Me habían examinado y no tengo el virus, soy negativo.

I am always careful.

Siempre tengo cuidado.

I always use a condom.

Siempre uso preservativos.

Siempre uso condones.

Sex is not worth it without a condom.

No vale el sexo sin preservativos/condones.

Horny	caliente
	cachondo
	velluco
(to) be Horny	estar caliente
	estar cachondo

(to) be Horny(cont.)   estar velluco

Oh, man I am so horny.

Ay, hombre estoy tan caliente.

Are you honry?   **¿Estás caliente?**

We are really honry.

Estamos muy cachondos.

He is always horny.

Él siempre está caliente.

Why are you so honry?

¿Por qué estás tan cachondo?

I need sex!!!!!   **Necesito sexo.**

Hole(asshole)	el agujero
	la cacha del culo
	el culo
	el hoyo
	el ojete
	el trasero
	el ano

Hunk	un guapetón
	un guapote
	un tío guapo

Man, he is a (fucking) hunk.

Hombre, él es un (pinhe) guapetón.

What a hunk.	**¡Qué guapo!**
	¡Qué guapote!
	¡Qué tío guapo!

(to) Hurt	**hacer daño/herir(ie)**
Don't hurt me!.	**¡No me hagas daño!**
He hurt me.	**Él me hizo daño.**
Oh, baby. Hurt me.	**¡Hazme daño. Baby!**

I am not going to hurt you.

No voy a hacerte daño (No te voy hacer daño).

When I fuck you, it won't hurt.

Cuando te cojo, no te la hace daño.

I will put it in slowly.   **Te la meto despacio.**

Be careful. I know it will hurt.

Ten cuidado. Yo sé que me la hace daño.

I am going to use enough lub that it won't hurt you.
Promise.**Voy a usar bastante lubricante y no te la hace daño. Te prometo.**

Hustler   **un chapero**

                           un gígalo

                           un chulo

...bar   **...un bar de chaperos**

...He's a hustler. Watch it.   **Él es chapero. Ten cuidado.**

...I like huslers.   **Me gustan los chaperos.**

...How much?   **¿Cuánto es? o ¿Cuánto cuesta?**

...That depends.   **Depende.**

...For you? Nothing.   **Para ti. Nada.**

Many hustlers are not gay.	**Muchos chaperos no son gay.**
They are gay of pay.	**Son gay por pago.**

Husband	**un marido**
	un esposo
…partner	**una pareja**

I don't have a partner.	**No tengo pareja.**

Do you have a partner?	**¿Tienes pareja?**
…boyfriend?	**¿… novio?**
…lover.	**¿… amante?**

I have a partner but we have an open relationship.

Tengo pareja pero tenemos relación abierta.

I have a boyfriend and we have an open relationship.

Tengo novio y tenemos relación abierta.

I am sorry but I'm not interested in guys that are in a relationship.

Lo siento pero no me interesan chavos que están en relaciones.

I want a honest relationship. I cannot share my man.

Quiero una relación honesta. No puedo compartir mi pareja.

I

Impotent   **impotente**

Impotence   **impotencia**

     I hear that he is impotent.

     Oigo que él es impotente.

That is true, he is.

Es verdad que él es impotente.

Will viagra help?	**¿Sirve viagra?**
Who knows?	**¿Quién sabe?**

Older men have problems with impotence.

Hombres maduros tienen problemas con impotencia.

Intercourse   **las relaciones sexuales (coger/follar)**

Intimacy   **la intimidad**

Intimate   **íntimo**

     I want to be intimate with you.

     Quiero estar íntimo contigo.

I like intimate relations.

Me gustan relaciones íntimas.

Let's be intimate.	**Estemos íntimos.**
He is my close friend.	**Él es mi amigo íntimo.**
We are close friends.	**Somos amigos íntimos.**

J

Jail bait	un menor
	un joven menor de la edad legal
He's jail bait.	Él es un menor.
I don't like 'kids'.	No me gustan los menores.
He is too young.	Él es demasiado joven.

I like men not 'kids'.

Me gustan los hombres, no los menores de edad.

Jealous	**celoso**
(to) be Jealous	**estar celoso**
We are not jealous.	**No estamos celosos.**

My boyfriend is very jealous. **Mi novio esta muy celoso.**

| I am not jealous. | **No estoy celoso.** |
| He used to be so jealous. | **Él estaba tan celoso.** |

I don't know why he is jealous.

No sé por qué él está celoso.

Don't be jealous.	**¡No estés celoso!**
Let's not be jealous.	**¡No estemos celosos!**
(to) be Jealous (to have Jealousy)	**tener celos**
I am jealous.	**Tengo celos.**
You are jealous.	**Tienes celos.**

I used to be jealous.   **Yo tenía celos.**

We were (used to be) jealous. **Teníamos celos.**

Jock   **un atleta**

                        un macho

   They are jocks.   **Ellos son atletas**

   He is a real jock.   **Él es un buen atleta.**

   He is a macho jock. **Él es un atleta macho.**

He thinks he's a macho.

Él piensa que es macho

   ..but he's as gay and you and I.

   ...pero es tan gay como tú y yo.

Jock strap   **un sorporte atlético**

   I like a guy who wears a jock strap.

   Me gusta un tío que lleva un sorporte.

I like to the smell of a a jock strap.

Me gusta el olor de un sorporte.

   I need to buy a jock strap.

   Necesito comprar un sorporte.

He is a nice package in that jock strap.

Tiene buen paquete en ese sorporte.

(to) Jump   **saltar**

    Jump on me. Baby.   **¡Sáltame! Papi**

    Jump on me and fuck me hard.   **¡Sáltame   y**
cójeme muy duro!

    I want you to jump my bones.

    Quiero que me saltes y me mames la pinga.

Don't jump my bones.   **¡No me saltes el palo!**

K

Kinky   **morboso**

                    vicioso

    He is kinky.   **Él es morboso/vicioso.**

I like a guy who is a little kinky.

Me gusta un tío que es un poco morboso.

    He has a lot of vices.   **Él tiene muchos vicios.**

 (to) Kiss   **besar**

a Kiss   **un beso**

a big Kiss   **un besote**

    I want to kiss you .   **Quiero besarte**

I want to kiss you on the lips. **Quiero besar los labios.**

    Do you like to kiss?   **¿Te gusta besar?**

Do you want to kiss me?	**¿Deseas besarme?**
Kiss me!	**¡Bésame!**
Kiss me a lot!	**¡Bésame mucho!**
Don't kiss me.	**¡No me beses!**
Kiss me on the lips.	**¡Bésame en los labios!**

Do you want to kiss/lick my sweet ass?

¿Quieres besar/lamer mi dulce culo?

Kiss my whole body.	**¡Besa todo mi cuerpo!**

(to) smoother with Kisses.   **Besuquear**

I want to smoother you with kisses.

Quiero besuquearte.

many smoothering kisses   **besuqueos**

I want to give you …

Quiero darte muchos busequeos.

(to) go to your Knees.   **arrodillarse**

I'll get on my knees to suck you big cock.

Me arrodillo para mamar tu verga grande.

I like to suck you on my knees.

Me gusta mámartela mientras estoy arrodillado.

Get on your knees and suck me.

¡Arrodíllate y chupámela!

¡Arrodíllate y mámamela!

On your knees.   **En las rodillas.**

                                  A las rodillas.

Get on your knees and put your tougue up my ass.

¡Arrodíllate y ponte tu lengua en mi culo!

Get on your knees and eat out my ass.

Arrodíllate y lámeme el hoyo/el culo.

Man. I got on my knees and suck him dry.

Hombre. Me arrodillé y me la mamé bien seca.

I like a guy on his knees sucking me off.

Me gusta un tío arrodillado, mamándomela.

I don't get on my knees for anybody.

No me arrodillo para nadie.

I will get on my knees for you baby.

Me arrodillo para ti baby.

L

A Lay/Fuck   **una follada**

                                  una cogida

Man, he is a good fuck.

Él es una buena follada/cogida.

He fucks great.

lla/coge muy bien.

He is a great fuck.

Él es una follada/cogida muy buena.

He fuck me so hard. **Él me folló tan fuerte.**

Él me cogió tan fuerte.

I fucked him doggie style. **Lo cogí a cuatro patas.**

Lo follé a lo bruto.

He was fucking me real hard and it hurt.

El estaba follando muy duro y me hizo daño.

I wanted him to fuck me again.

Quería que me follara/cogiera otra vez.

You want a good lay?

¿Quieres una buena follada?

You want to fuck me? **¿Quieres cogerme?**

¿Quieres follarme?

Leather **el cuero**

la piel

He's a cowboy and wears leather.

Él es vaquero y lleva el cuero/la piel.

He's into leather.

A él le gusta el cuero.

Libido   **el libido**

(to) Lick/rim   **lamerle (el culo)**

I want to lick your balls.

Quiero lamerte los huevos.

I want to rim your hot ass.

Quiero lamerte el culo caliente.

Lick my cock.   **¡Lámeme la polla/la verga!**

Lick my balls.   **Lámeme las pelotas/los huevos!**

Suck my balls. **¡Chúpame los huevos/las pelotas!**

    Lick'me.   **¡Lámelos o Lámelas!**

    Eat me out.   **¡Lámemelo!**

    Eat it all.   **¡Cómetelo entero!**

I like to be eaten out.   **Me gusta el beso negro.**

a Lick   **un lametón**

(to) Like   **gustarle**

    I like you.   **Me gustas.**

I like you the way you are. **Me gustas tal como eres.**

    Do you like me?   **¿Me gustas?**

    I like to be with you. **Me gusta estar.**

I like your cock.   **Me gusta tu verga/polla/pinga.**

I like to suck.   **Me gusta mamar/chupar.**

I don't like to be fucked...**No me gusta estar follado/cogido.**

Do you like to kiss?   **¿Te gusta besar?**

Do you like to cuddle? **¿Te gusta acariciar?**

Do you like to hug?   **¿Te gusta abrazar?**

Do you like to rim?   **¿Te gusta lamer?**

I would like...   **Me gustaría...**

I would like to fuck you.   **Me gustaría follarte/cogerte.**

I would like to be your boyfriend...**Me gustaría ser tu novio.**

What do you like to do sexually?

¿Qué te gusta hacer dssexualmente?

What do you like to do in bed?

¿Que te gusta hacer en la cama?

I like it all.   **Me gusta todo.**

Did you like it?   **¿Te gustó?**

Yes, I liked it a lot.   **Sí, me gustó mucho**

I like it and he fucked me again.

Me gustó y me folló, otra vez.

(to) Love   **Querer**(ie) a

    Amar (serious business)

Do you love me?	**¿Me quieres?**
Yes, I love you.	**Sí, te quiero**
Do you love him?	**¿Lo quieres?**
No, I don't love him.	**No, no lo quiero.**
Do you love?	**¿Me amas?**
Yes, I love you.	**Sí, te amo.**

I love you very much.	**Te amo mucho.**
I love you more than anything.	**Te amo más que nada.**
You do love me. Don't you?	**Me amas. ¿verdad?**

Love	**querido**
	amor
You are my love.	**Eres mi amor.**
	Eres mi querido.

My love(dear). I love you so much.

Mi querido, te amo tanto.

Mi amor, te quiero tanto.

You are my true love.	**Eres mi amor verdadero.**
	Eres mi querido verdadero.

I believe in love at first site.

Creo en el amor a la primera vista.

I am a romantic and I believe in love.

Soy romántico y creo en el amor.

I am a lover.   **Soy amante.**

(to) be in Love   **estar enamorado.**

I am in love with you.

Estoy enamorado de ti.

Are you in love with me.

¿Estás enamorado de mí?

We are in love.   **Estamos enamorados.**

We were in love.   **Estábamos enamorados.**

I am in love with him.   **Estoy enamorado de él.**

I don't love you anymore.   **No te quiero más.**

(to) Fall in Love.   **enamorarse de**

I am falling in love with you . **Me enamoro de ti.**

I am falling in love with him.   **Me enamoro de él.**

We are falling in love.   **Nos enamoramos.**

Don't fall in love with him.   **¡No te enamores de él!**

Fall in love with me!   **¡Enamórate de mí!**

The first time I saw you. I fell in love.

La primera vez que te vi, me enamoré.

(to) Fall in Love   **enamorarse de**

I fell in love with you the first time I saw you.

Me enamoré de ti la primera vez que te vi.

Did you fall in love with me the first time you saw me?

¿Me enamoraste la primera vez que me viste?

Did you fall in love with him?

¿Te enamoraste de él?

We fell in love right then.

Nos enamoramos al inmediato.

Love at first site.	**el amor a la primera vista**
Love affair	**un romance**
	una aventura de amor
Love letter	**una carta de amor**
Love poem	**un poema de amor**
Love song	**una canción de amor**
(to make) Love	**hacer el amor**

I want to make love to you.

Quiero hacer el amor contigo.

I make love.	**Hago el amor.**
I make love with him.	**Hice el amor con él**
I make love to you.	**Hice el amor contigo.**
I was making love.	**Hacía el amor.**
	Estaba haciendo el amor.

Let's make love.   **¡Hagamos el amor!**

Having sex is not making love.

El hacer de sexo no es el hacer de amor.

Do you want to make love or have sex?

¿Quieres hacer el amor o hacer sexo?

I want to make love all night.

Quiero hacer el amor toda la noche.

Love handles	**los michelines**
Lover	**un amante**
	un novio

Do you have a lover?   **¿Tienes novio?**

                                      ¿Tienes amante?

Yes, I have a boyfriend.   **Sí, tengo novio.**

                                      Sí, tengo amante.

Lover	**un amante**
	un novio

I have a lover but we have an open relationship.

Tengo amante pero tenemos relación abierta.

I have a partner and we have an open relationship.

Tengo pareja y tenemos relación abierta.

That muscular guy is my lover.

Ese hombre musculoso es mi amante.

That handsome guy is my lover.

Ese hombre guapo es mi novio.

That sexy guy is my partner.

Ese hombre sexy es mi pareja.

I don't have an open relationship and I wouldn't want to share my man with anyone.

No tengo relación abierta y no podría compartir mi pareja con nadie.

What a lover you are my love.

¡Qué amante eres mi amor!

Loving	amoroso
	cariñoso
My man is so loving.	**Mi amor es tan amoroso.**
	Mi hombre es tan cariñoso.
He is so loving.	**Él es tan amoroso.**
We are a loving couple.	**Somos pareja amorosa.**
You are so loving baby.	**Eres tan amoroso. Papi.**

You are so affectionate my love.

Eres tan cariñoso mi querido.

(to be) Love sick for   **estar enfermo de amor por**

I am love sick for you baby.

Estoy enfermo de amor por ti, mi nene.

He is so love sick for that jock.

Él está enfermo de amor por ese atleta.

Lust/wish   **un deseo**
                             una lujuria
                             una lascivia

He has a lust for muscular men.

Él tiene una lujuria por hombres musculosos.

I have a lust for beautiful men.

Tengo un deseo por hombres bellos.

We are lustfull for hot men.

Tenemos lascivia por hombre calientes.

(to) Lust (desire/wish/want)   **desear**

I desire you a lot.   **Te deseo mucho.**

Do you desire me?   **¿Me deseas?**

125

He is a desire/wish.   **Él es un deseo.**

M

(to be on the) Make   **estar de ligue**

    I am on the make for a hot man..

    Estoy de ligue con un hombre caliente.

Are you on the make again?

¿Estás de ligue otra vez?

Man/men   **el hombre**

                                    los hombres

big Man   **el hombre grande**

                                      el hombretón

fat Man   **el hombre gordo**

slinder Man   **el hombre delgado**

skinny Man   **el hombre flaco**

muscular Man   **el hombre musculoso**

handsome Man   **el hombre guapo/hermoso**

beautiful Man   **el hombre bello**

fine Man   **el hombre fino**

viril Man   **el hombre viril**

macho Man	**el hombre macho**
gay Man	**el hombre gay**
masculine Man	**el hombre masculino**
Manly	**la virilidad**
	varonil
	de varón
Massage	**un masaje**

I need a massage.   **Necesito masaje.**

I need a full massage.   **Necesito masaje total**

I want a sexual massage.   **Quiero un masaje sexual.**

I need a massage to relax.

Necesito masaje para relajarme.

(to) give/do Massage	**dar masaje**
	masajear

Give me a massage.   **¡Dame masaje!**

I am going to give you a great massage.

Voy a darte un masaje maravilloso.

Take your clothes for the massage.

¡Quítate la ropa para el masaje!

(to) give/ Massage	**dar masaje**
	masajear

I have a towel to cover you.

Tengo toalla para cubrirte.

A good massage will relax you.

Un buen masaje va a relajarte.

A stemulating massage is heavenly.

Un masaje estimulante es regalo desde el cielo.

I will massage your cock.

Voy a masajear tu polla.

Do you like the cock massage.

¿Te gusa el masaje de la polla?

Massage it with your mouth.

¡Masajéala con tu boca!

Massage my buttocks with your hands.

¡Masajea las nalgas con tus manos!

Massage my ass with a finger.

¡Masejea el culo con un dedo!

How much is a good massage?

¿Cuánto cuesta un buen masaje?

It's cost $50 per hour?

Cuesta cincuenta dólares por hora

For a sexual full release massage?

¿Para un sexual masaje full de descarga?

$150 per hour.

Ciento cincuenta dólares por hora.

I need a neck massage.

Necesito masaje del cuello.

I need a shoulder massage.

Necesito masaje de los hombros.

I need a leg massage.

Necesito masaje de las piernas.

I need a dick/cock massage.

Necesito masaje de polla/verga.

I need an foot massage.

Necesito masaje de los pies.

Masseur   **masajista**

You are a good masseur.

Eres buen masajista.

He is a good looking masseur.

Él es masajista guapo.

He is a sexy masseur.

Él es masajista sexy.

He is an excellent masseur

Él masajista excelente.

Master   **el amo**

                            el señor

         master and slave   **El amo y esclavo**

(to) Masterbate   **masturbarse**

I like to masterbate 3 times a day.

Me gusta masturbarme tres veces al día.

      I masterbate a lot.

      Me masturbo mucho.

I'm masterbating.

Me estoy masturbando

(to) Masterbate   **masturbarse**

      Let's masterbate.

      ¡Masturbémonos!

      ¡Vamos a masturbarnos!

      Let's masterbate together.   ¡

      Vamos a masturbarnos juntos!

      ¡Masturbémonos juntos!

We only masterbated.

Sólo nos masturbamos.

Did you masterbate last night?

¿Te masturbaste anoche?

Yes, I did and it was great.

Sí, me masturbé y fue tremendo.

I masterbated 3 times this morning.

Me masturbé tres veces esta mañana.

Don't masterbate so much.

No te masturbas tanto.

My dick gets bigger when I masterbate a lot

Mi polla se pone más grande cuando me masturbo.

If you want, I will masterbate you.

Si quieras, te masturbo.

Go ahead. Masterbate me.   **¡Adelante, mastúrbamela!**

Meat   **la carne**

131

I would like your cock in my mouth.

Me gustaría tu carne en la boca.

Would you like my big cock.

¿Te gusta mi carne grande?

| Meat market/rack | **una carnicería** |
| | **un picadero** |

Damn. This place is a meat market.

Hombre, este lugar es una carnicería.

Hombre, este sitio es un picadero.

| Mostly hustlers. | **La mayoría chaperos.** |

They are standing around the bar wanting to be picked up. Sex for pay.

Están alrededor de la barra para salir con alguien para el sex y por pago.

The beach is like a meat rack.

La playa es como un picadero/una carnicería.

| (to) Molest/abuse | **abusar** |
| Molester | **abusador** |

He's a molester of children.

Él es abusador de niños.

I don't like child molesters.

No me gustan abusadores de niños.

Monogamous   **monógamo**

     I am in a monogamous relation.

     Estoy en relación monógama.

We are in a monogamous relation.

Estamos en relación monógama.

     I am monogamous.

     Estoy monógamo.

We are monogamous.

Estamos monógamo.

     I am monogamous and I do not cheat.

     Estoy monógamo y no engaño.

We are monogamous and we don't cheat.

Estamos monógmos y no nos engañamos.

(to) Mount   **montar**

     I want to fuck you.   **Quiero follarte.**

     I want to mount you.   **Quiero montarte.**

Mount me and fuck me strong.

¡Móntame y fóllame bien fuerte!

     Mount me and pound my ass hard!

     ¡Montame y clávame el culo bien fuerte.

| You want to mount me? | ¿Quieres montarme? |

Mouth	la boca
Use your mouth.	¡Usa tu boca!
Put it in your mouth	¡Póntela en tu boca!
…and suck it hard.	…y mámala muy fuerte.
Put my ball in your mouth.	¡Ponte las pelotas en tu boca!
I want to cum in your mouth.	Quiero venir en tu boca.
	Quiero acabar en tu boca.
	Quiero correrme en tu boca.

I want to fill your mouth with my cum and you can swallow it all
Quiero llenar la boca con mi leche y puede tragarla toda.

You want me to cum in your mouth?
¿Quieres que yo venga en tu boca?

Do you want to cum in my mouth?
¿Quieres que yo acabe en tu boca?
¿Quieres que yo me corra en tu boca?

Cum in my mouth.	¡Ven en mi boca!
	¡Acaba en mi boca!
	¡Córrete en mi boca.

Mouth	**la boca**
Don't cum in my mouth.	**¡No vengas en mi boca!**
	¡No acabes en mi boca!
	¡No te corras en mi boca!

(to) Nail/Drive in	**clavar**
Drive it in(fuck me).	**¡Clávame!**
	¡Clávamela!
Drive it in hard.	**¡Clávame muy fuerte!**
I want to drive it in hard.	**Quiero clavarte muy fuerte.**

Nipple	**el pezón**
Nipples	**los pezones**

Suck my nipples.   **¡Chupa mis pezones!**

You make me hot when you suck my nipples.
Me pone caliente cuando me chupas los pezones.

I love to suck nipples.

Me gusta chupar pezones.

Can I suck your nipples?

¿Puedo chupar tus pezones?

Nipple clamp	**una pinza**
Nipple ring	**un anillo**
	un pendiente
Nude	**desnudo**
(to be) Nude	**estar desnudo**

I am naked.	**Estoy desnudo.**
Are you nude?	**¿Estás desnudo?**

I would like to see you naked/nude.

Me gustaría verte desnudo.

I like being nude/naked.

Me gusta estar desnudo.

(to get) Naked/Nude	**desnudarse**
I am getting naked for you.	**Me desudo para ti.**
Let's get naked.	**¡Vamos a desnudarnos!**

(to get) Naked/Nude	**desnudarse**
Let's get naked!	**¡Desnúdemonos!**
Get naked!	**¡Desnúdate!**
I want to take my clothes off.	**Quiero desnudarme.**
	Quiero quitarme la ropa.
Take your clothes off.	**¡Quítate la ropa!**

Nude beach	una playa desuda
	una playa nudista
	una playa naturalista
Nudist	un nudista
Nudist colony	una colonia nudista
Nudity	la desnudez

O

One night stand **un rollo de un día**

> I don't want a one night stand.
>
> **No quiero un rollo de un día.**

| I want more (than that). | **Quiero más.** |
| I only want a one nighter. | **Sólo quiero un rollo.** |

Orgasm	**orgasmo**
hot orgasm	**orgasmo caliente**
(to have) Orgasm	**tener orgasmo**
I am having an orgasm.	**Tengo orgasmo.**
Orgasmic	**orgásmico**
hot orgasmic love	**un caliente amor orgásmico**
hot orgasmic sex	**sexo caliente orgásmico**
Orgy	**una orgía**
Do you like orgies?	**¿Te gustan orgías?**
Yes, I love orgies.	**Sí, me encantan orgías.**
Let's have an orgy!	**Vamos a tener una orgía.**

| | ¡Tengamos una orgía! |
| We love orgies. | Nos encantan orgías. |

| He loves going to orgies. | A él le gusta asistir a orgías. |
| You want to go to an orgy? | ¿Quiere asistir a una orgía? |

Oversexed	**dispardo**
	desatado
He is so oversexed.	**Él es tan destado/dispardo.**
I need a lot of sex.	**Necesito mucho sexo.**
We are so oversexed.	**Somos tan destados/dispardos.**
We need a lot of sex.	**Necesitamos mucho sexo.**

P

Package	**paquete**
(big) Package	**paquetote**
	paquete grande
	regalo
You have a big package.	**Tienes un buen paquetote.**

I have a big package for you.

Tengo un buen paquetote para ti.

I like your package.	**Me gusta tu paquete.**
You have a nice package.	**Tienes buen regalo.**
Pain	**dolor**
	pena
I don't like pain.	**No me gusta pena.**

(to have) Pain **tener dolor de...**

I have an headache.

Tengo dolor de la cabeza.

I have a stomach ache.

Tengo dolor del estómago

Does your leg hurt? **¿Tienes dolor de la pierna?**

(to) hurt/have Pain **dolerle**

My ass hurts. **Me duele el culo.**

My neck hurts after sucking you for an hour.

Me duele el cuello después de mamarte por una hora.

My cock/penis hurts. **Me duele el pene**

(to) hurt/have Pain **dolerle**

Does your hand hurt? **¿Te duele la mano?**

My finger hurts.	**Me duele el dedo.**	
Does it hurt?	**¿Te duele?**	
	¿Tienes dolor/pena?	
Partner	**pareja**	
Partners	**parejas**	
He is my partner.	**Él es mi pareja.**	
Do you have a partner?	**¿Tienes pareja?**	
We are partners	**Somos pareja.**	
Party	**una fiesta**	
	una parranda	
	una pachanga	
Let's go to a party.	**¡Vamos a una fiesta!**	

(to go) Party	**ir de parranda**	
	parrandear	
Let's go party.	**¡Vamos de parranda!**	
	¡Vamos a parrandear!	
I don't like to party.	**No me gusta ir de parranda.**	
	No me gusta parrandear.	
Partier	**un parrandeo**	
He is a partier.	**Él es parrandeo.**	
I am not a partier.	**No soy parrandeo.**	
We were partiers.	**Éramos parrandeos.**	
He was a partier.	**Él era parrandeo.**	

Passion   **pasión**

     with a lot of passion   **con mucha pasión**

     a kiss of passion   **un beso con pasión**

Passionate   **apasionado**

(to be) Passionate   **estar apasionado**

     I am very passionate now.   **Ahora estoy muy apasionado.**

     We are very passionate from time to time.   **De vez en cuando estamos muy apasionados.**

     He is passionate.   **Él es apasionado.**

     We are passionate.   **Somos apasionados.**

     Don't be so passionate.   **¡No seas tan apasionado!**

Passive/bottom   **pasivo**

     Are you a bottom?   **¿Eres pasivo?**

     I am a bottom   **Soy pasivo.**

     Are you a top/active)   **¿Eres activo?**

     He is a top.   **Él es activo**

     He is both.   **Él es versatil.**

     He's more of a bottom.   **Él es más pasivo.**

(to) Pee/piss/urinate   **mear**

                         urinar

                         hacer pis pis

	pasar agua
I have to piss	**Tengo que mear.**
	Tengo que urinar
	Tengo que hacer pis pis
He went to piss.	**Él fue a mear.**
	Él fue a urinar
Can I piss in your mouth?	**¿Puedo mear en tu boca?**

No, I am not into water sports.

No, no me interesa deportes de agua.

(to) Penetrate   **penetrar**

I want to penetrate you.	**Quiero penetrarte.**
Put it in me.	**¡Penétramela!**
Don't put it in me.	**¡No me penetres!**

I want to penetrate your tight ass.

Quiero penetrar tu culo apretado

Penis   **el pene**

I like your penis.	**Me gusta tu pene.**
Wow, You have a large penis.	**Wow, tienes un pene grande.**
I love big penises.	**Me gustan penes grandes.**
You have a nice penis.	**Tienes un buen pene.**

Pervert	**el pervertido**
He is a pervert.	**Él es pervertido.**
He is a sick pervert.	**Él es pervertido enfermo.**
They are perverts.	**Ellos son pervertidos.**
I don't like sexual perverts..	
No me gustan pervertido sexuales.	
They are sick.	**Son enfermos.**

(to) Pet/caress	**acariciarse**
I want to caress you.	**Quiero acariciarte.**
Caress me.	**¡Acaríciame!**
Phallic	**fálico**
Phallic symbol	**símbolo fálico**
Phallic sign	**signo fálico**
Phallus	**el falo**

Piercings	**perforaciones**
...body piercings	**anillos del cuerpo**
(to have) body Piercings	
tener anillos del cuerpo	
He has body piercings.	
Él tiene anillos del cuerpo.	

Do you have body piercings?

¿Tienes anillos del cuerpo?

    I don't have piercings.   **No tengo anillos.**

(to) Play   **jugar**(ue)

    Do you like to play?   **¿Te gusta jugar?**

    I like to play.   **Me gusta jugar.**

    Do you play?   **¿Juegas?**

    Play with me.   **¡Juega conmigo!**

    Don't play with me.   **¡No juegues conmigo!**

    Let's play.   **¡Vamos a jugar1**

                                ¡Juguemos!

    I used to play.   **Yo jugaba.**

    We used to play.   **Jugábamos**

    Do you want to play?   **¿Quieres jugar?**

    I will play with you.   **Voy a jugar contigo.**

Play thing.   **un juguete**

                        un juguetón

    Be my play thing!   **¡Sea mi juguete!**

    He's a play thing.   **Él es un jagueón.**

    I'm not your play thing.   **No soy tu juguete.**

I am not somebody who is a play thing.

No soy alguien que es un juguetón.]

Pleasure   **el placer**

     I want to give you pleasure.

     Quiero darte placer.

I would like to give you pleasure.

Me gustaría darte placer.

Pleasure   **el placer**

     It is a pleasure.   **Es un placer.**

I like pleasure not pain.

Me gusta el placer no el dolor.

     Do you want to make love to me?

     ¿Te gusta hacer el amor conmigo?

It would be a pleasure.

Sería un placer.

     It is a pleasure to know you.

     Es un placer en conocerte.

What a pleasure!   **¡Qué placer!**

Porn   **el porno**

Pornographic   **pornográfico**

Pornography   **pornografía**

I like to fuck with porno.   **Me gusta follar con porno.**

Do you like porn?		¿Te gusta el porno?
No, I don't.		No, no me gusta.
I like it a lot.		Me gusta mucho
Precum	el goteo	
	el flujo	
Promiscuous	pro<u>mis</u>cuo	
Prostitute(male)	puto	
	prostituto	
	chapero	
	gígalo	
What a whore!		¡Qué puto!
He's a fucking hustler.		Él es un pinche chapero.
He's a fucking whore		Él es un pinche puto.
He used to be a whore.		Él era un prostituto.

(to) Punish	castigar	
I am going to punish you.		Voy a castigarte.
Don't punish me!		¡No me castigues!
Punish me!		¡Castígame!

Punishment	el castigo	

There is punishment to have sex with a minor.

Hay un castigo de hacer sexo con un menor.

146

It's not worth it.

No vale la pena.

Q

Queen	**una loca**
	una reina
Queer	**maricón**
	marica
	mariposa
	joto
size Queen	**una falocrática**
Quickie	**un quickie**
	un polvo rápido
(to have) a Quickie	**echar un polvo rápido**
	echar un quicki

(to have/do) a Quickie	**hacer un quickie**
(to give) a Quickie	**dar un quickie**

Give me a quickie.	**¡Dame un quickie!**
	¡Échame un quickie!
	¡Hazme un polvo rápido!

I don't do quickies.	**No hago quickies.**
	No doy quickies.
	No echo polvos rápidos.

R

Rape	**la violación**
(to) Rape	**violar**

He raped me.	**Él me violó.**
He is going to rape me.	**Él va a violarme.**
I am going to rape you.	**Voy a violarte.**

(to) gang Rape	**violar en grupo/colectiva**
Rapist	**el violador**
Rectum	**el recto**
Relationship	**una relación**

serious relationship	**una relación seria**
open relationship	**una relación abierta**
platonic relatinship	**una relación platónica**
bad/good relationship	**una mala/buena relación**

(to) Rim	**lamerle el culo**
I am going to give you a rim job.	**Voy a lamerte el culo.**
Are you going to rim me?	**¿Vas a lamérmelo?**

I like to give you rim jobs.	**Me gusta lamerte el culo.**
Lick me with your tougue.	**Lámeme con tu lengua.**

Romantic	**romántico**
I am a romantic.	**Soy romántico.**
I hope you are a romantic.	**Espero que seas romántico.**

We are romantics.	**Somos románticos.**
A hopeless romantic.	**Un romántico sin esperanza.**
A hopefull romantic.	**Un romántico con esperanza.**

Romance	**un romance**
Rough	**a lo duro**
	a lo bruto

I like rough sex.	**Me gusta sexo a lo bruto.**
Do you like rough sex?	**¿Te gusta el sexo a lo duro?**
Do you want rough sex?	**¿Quieres sexo a lo bruto?**
Yes, ride me baby.	**Sí, ¡móntame nene!**
Rough trade	**…de la clase baja**
He's rough trade.	**Él es de la clase baja.**
I don't like rough trade.	

No me gusta hombres de la clase baja.

S

Sadism	**el sadismo**
Sadist	**el sádico**
Sadomasochism	**el sado masoquismo**
Sadomasochistic	**el sado masquista**
S & M	**sado-maso**

He likes S & M.

A él le gusta sado-maso (eSe-eMe).

I don't like S & M.

No me gusta sado-maso (eSe-eMe).

He used to be sadmasochistic.

Él era sado masquista.

He likes to fist fuck.

A él le gusta coger/follar con el puño.

He is so dominate.	**Él es muy dominante.**
100% top.	**Ciento por ciento activo.**

He likes to be on top. **Él quiere dominar.**

He like to be in control and be dominate.

Él quiere estar en control y ser dominante.

Safe sex   **el sexo seguro**

Today it is important to have safe sex.

Hoy es importante tener sexo seguro.

Be smart and only have safe sex.

Sea inteligente y sólo tenga sexo seguro.

Life is to short not to have safe sex.

La vida es muy corta de no tener sexo seguro.

I only practice safe sex.

Sólo practico sexo seguro.

Practice safe sex and use a condom.

¡Practique sexo seguro, use un condón!

I am not easy if I use a condom. It is the smart thing to do.

No soy fácil si uso un condón. Es la cosa inteligente para hacer.

The use of condoms protects you and your partner.

El uso de condones te protege y a tu pareja.

I use a condom during oral sex.

Uso un condón durante sexo oral.

The HIV virus can enter the body through small cuts in the mouth. Be careful. Practice Safe Sex.
El virus VIH puede entrar al cuerpo a través de cortaduras en la boca. Tenga Cuidado.

When a guy says he will not have sex without a condom. Great.
Cuando un tío dice que no tendrá sexo sin un condón, Está Bien.

Because he wants to protect himself from diseases. And that s intellegent.
Porque necesita protegerse de las enfermedades. Y es inteligente.

Without safe sex, you are putting your life at risk. It is dangerous and it is not worth it.
Sin el uso de sexo seguro, estás poniéndote en riesco. Es peligoso y no vale la pena.

Be Intelligent!   Always use a condom.
¡SEA INTELIGENTE!   ¡SIEMPRE USE CONDÓN!

Seduce	**seducir**
Seduction	**la seducción**
Seductive	**seductivo**
Seducer	**el seductor**
Seman	**el semen**
	la esperma
Shaved/Smooth	**afeitado**

(to)Shave   **afeitarse**

    He is shaved.   **Él es afeitado**

    I am smooth.   **Soy afeitado y suave.**

S

(Cont.)

He shaves his balls.   **Él se afeita los huevos.**

Let me shave your balls.   **¡Déjame afeitar los huevos!**

    I like guys who shave the nuts.

Me gustan hombres con pelotas afeitadas

Smooth   **suave**

    smooth or hairy   **suave o velludo/peludo**

Shit   **la mierda**

                     la caca

(to) Shit   **cagar**

    I have to take a shit. **Tengo que cagar.**

    I don't eat shit.   **No como la mierda.**

    I don't care for it.   **No la quiero.**

After he fucked me I had to shit.

Después de follarme, tenía que cagar.

(to) Shower   **ducharse**

                    bañarse

Before sex, let's shower.

Antes de sexo, ¡vamos a bañarnos!

Antes de sexo, ¡báñemonos!

Antes de sexo, ¡vamos a ducharnos!

Antes de sexo, ¡vamos a tomar una ducha!

I have to douche my ass.

Tengo que duchar el culo.

I want to be good and clean.

Quiero estar bien limpio.

Sister	**hermana**
Single	**soltero**

Are you single?	**¿Eres soltero?**
Is he single?	**¿Es soltero?**
I am single and available.	**Soy soltero y disponible.**
Slap	**una bofetada**
(to) Slap	**dar una bofetada.**

I am going to slap you .	**Voy a darte una bofetada.**
Don't slap me.	**¡No me des una bofetada!**
Give me a slap.	**¡Dame una bofetada!**

He slapped me.	**Me dio una bofetada.**
Slave	**un esclavo**

Sex Slave   **un esclavo sexula/un esclavo de sexo**

You want to be my sex slave?

¿Quieres ser mi esclavo sexula?

I want to be your sex slave.

Quiero ser tu esclavo de sexo.

I am your master and you are my slave.

Soy tu amo y eres mi esclavo.

I will do what you want.

Hago lo que quieras.

He is my sex slave.

Él es mi esclavo de sexo.

Sleaze   **un vicioso**

He is such a sleaze.   **Él es tan vicioso.**

I am not a sleaze.   **No soy vicioso.**

He is a fucking sleaze bitch.   **Él un pinche puto vicioso.**

(to) Sleep around   **ir de cama en cama.**

I sleep around.   **Voy de cama en cama.**

He always sleeps around.   **Siempre va de cama en cama.**

He used to sleep around.   **Él iba de cama en cama.**

He goes from guy to guy.   **Él va de hombre en hombre.**

                             Él va de tío en tío.

He goes from one queer to another.

Él va de una marica en marica.

> **....de un maricón en maricón.**

> **....de un joto en joto.**

He goes from cock to another.   **Él va de una polla en polla.**

> **.......de una verga en verga.**

> **.......de un pito den pito.**

(to) Sleep   **dormir**(ue)

> Who do you sleep with?   **¿Con quién duermes?**

> I sleep with Carlos.   **Duermo con Carlos.**

> Are you sleeping with José?   **¿Duermes con José?**

Yes, because he a has big dick.

Sí, duermo con José porque tiene una pinga grande.

> I sleep with him because he is a good cocksucker.

Duermo con él porque es una buena chupapolla

(to) Sleep   **dormir**(ue)

> Do you want to sleep with me ?

> **¿Quieres dormir conmigo?**

Can I sleep with you?   **¿Puedo dormir contigo?**

> Yes, you can.   **Sí, puedes dormir conmigo?**

Do you want to go to bed with me?

¿Quieres acostarte conmigo?

Yes, I want to go to bed with you.

Sí, quiero acostarme contigo.

Go to be with me!   **¡Acuéstate conmigo!**

Let's go to bed together.   **¡Vamos a acostarnos juntos!**

¡Acostémonos, juntos!

Can I make love to you?   **¿Puedo hacer el amor contigo?**

Yes, you can.   **Sí, puedes hacer el amor conmigo.**

(to) Spank   **pegar las nalgas**

Spank me!   **¡Pégame!**

I want a daddy who will spank me.

Quiero un tío que me pegues

Spank me daddy.   **¡Pégame papi, pégame!**

Are you going to spank me?   **¿Vas a pegarme?**

¿Me vas a pegar?

(to) Spread(open)   **abrir**

Spread your legs baby   **¡Abre las piernas baby!**

Spread your legs and let me fuck you.

¡Abre las piernas y déjame follarte!

I want you to spread your legs more.

Quiero que abras las piernas más.

I opened my ass for you .

Abrí el culo para ti.

(no) Strings attached

sin condiciones

sin compromisos

sin rollos

(to) Strip

estrip tease

 (to)Strip

desnudarse

Strip for me.

¡Desnúdate para mí!

I am going to strip for you.

Voy a desnudarme para ti.

Don't strip.

¡No te desnudes!

(to) Stick it in/put into

meter

Stick it in me.

¡Métemela!

Stick it in me deep.

¡Métemela al fondo!

Stick it in me hard.

¡Métemela a lo bruto/a lo duro/fuerte!

I want you to put it in me.

Quiero que me la metas.

I am going to put it up your tight ass.

Voy a metértela arriba tu culo apretado.

You want me to stick it up your tight ass.

Quieres que yo te la meta arriba tu culo apretado.

(to) Suck	**mamar**
	chupar
Suck me.	**¡Mámame!**
Suck me.	**¡Chúpame!**
Suck me off.	**¡Mámamela/chúpamela!**
Suck my dick	**¡Mama mi pinga!**
	mi verga!
	mi polla!
	mi rábano!
Suck it.	**¡Mámala/Chúpala!**
Suck the dick!	**¡Mama la verga!**
	la pinga!
	la polla!
	el palo!
	el pito!
Suck my nipples.	**¡Chupa los pezones!**
I want to suck you.	**Quiero mamarte/chuparte.**
I want to suck you off.	**Quiero mamártela/chupártela.**

S

(to) Suck   **mamar**

                             chupar

Can I suck you off/   **¿Puedo mamártela?**

Yes, please suck me off.

Sí, Por favor. Mámamela.

Yes, you can suck me all night.

Sí, puedes mamarme toda la noche.

I like to suck it.

Me gusta mamarla/chuparla.

Do you like to suck?

¿Te gusta mamar?

I would like to suck your big cock.

Me gustaría mamar tu vergón/ tu verga grande.

When you suck, do you swallow?

Cuando mames, ¿la tragas?

I always swallow.

Siempre la trago.

Sugar daddy   **bomboncito**

                           papacito

                           papi

                           papi chulo

                           protector

I want a sugar daddy to take care of me.

Deseo un papacito para cuidarme.

You are my sugar daddy.

Eres mi bomboncito.

(to) Swallow **tragar**

I want to swallow your cum.

Deseo tragar tu leche.

I don't swallow. **No la trago.**

Swallow it baby. **¡Trágala baby!**

(to) Sweat **sudar**

Sweat **el sudor**

I like to lick your sweat off your cock and balls.

Me gusta lamer el sudor de tu polla y pelotas.

I like the sweet of a man.

Me gusta el sudor de un hombre.

I love to sweet when having hot sex.

Me encanta sudarme cuando hago sexo caliente.

I sweat a lot when I am fucking you.

Sudo mucho cuando estoy follándote.

(to) Sweat   **sudar**

I sweat a lot when I am sucking you .

Sudo mucho cuando estoy mamándote.

Sweat of my cock and balls.

El sudor/el aroma de mi polla y huevos.

You like?	¿Te gusta?
Sweet	**dulce**
Sweet cock	**verga dulce**
	polla dulce
	dulce verga
	dulce polla
Sweet ass	*dulce culo*
	culo dulce

You have a sweet ass.   **Tienes un dulce culo.**

...sweet cock.   **una dulce polla.**

...a delicious cock   **una deliciosa verga.**

                             una pinga deliciosa.

What a sweet cock!   **¡Qué verga tan dulce!**

....delicious cock!   **...tan deliciosa!**

162

What a delicious big cock!

¡Qué polla grande y deliciosa!

(my) Sweetheart/love/dear/heart/life	**mi amor/amor mío**
(terms of endearment)	**mi cariño**
	mi corazón/el corazón de mi vida
	mi querido/querido mío

(great terms of endearment)	my love	**mi amo**
	my affecionate one	**mi cariño**

my heart	**mi corazón**
my dear	**mi querido**

my life	**mi vida**
my reason for being	**mi razón de ser**
my doll baby	**mi muñeco**

the heart of my life.	**el corazón de mi vida**
my super man	**mi super hombre**
the love of my life	**el amor de mi vida**

T

Tender	**tierno**
Tenderly	**tiernamente**
Tenderness	**ternura**
a tender kiss	**un beso tierno**
a tender hug	**un abrazo tierno**
I treat you with tenderness.	**Te trato con ternura.**
Treat me with tenderness.	**¡Trátame con ternura!**
I kiss you tenderly.	**Te beso tiernamente**
	...con ternura.

We treat each other tenderly. **Nos tratamos con ternura.**

Strong hugs and tender kisses.

Con fuertes abrazos y besos tiernos.

Ah! How tender!   **¡Ah, qué tierno! ¡Qué ternura.**

Testicules	**los testículos**

He has large testicules.	**Él tiene testículos grandes.**
You have big balls.	**Tienes huevos grandes.**
I had testicular cancer.	**Tuve cáncer de los testículos.**

I survived the cancer.   **Sobreviví del cáncer.**

But, I only have one testicule.   **Pero, sólo tengo un testículo.**

And I have no sexual problem.

Y no tengo ningún problema sexual.

Three way   **un trío**

     Do you want to have a three way?

     ¿Quieres hacer un trío?

I don't like three ways.   **No me gustan los tríos.**

     I don't like to share my man with anyone.

     No me gusta compartir mi tío con nadie.

Throat   **la garganta**

     Suck my dick down your throat.

     ¡Mama mi verga dentro tu garganta!

You have a deep throat.

Tienes garganta profunda.

(to) Tie-up	**atar**
Tie me up!	**¡Átame!**
Put the handcuffs on.	**¡Ponme las esposas!**
Don't tie me up	**¡No me ates!**
Tie me to the bed.	**¡Átame a la cama!**
Blindfold me!	**¡Ponme una bendada!**
(to) unTie	**desatar**
Untie me.	**¡Desátame!**
Don't untie me!	**¡No me desates!**
Together	**juntos**
Let's live together.	**¡Vamos a vivir juntos!**
Tongue	**la lengua**
long tongue	**una lengua larga**
big tongue	**una lengua grande**
Use your tongue.	**¡Usa tu lengua!**

Put your tongue up my ass.

¡Mete tu lengua arriba mi culo!

Top	**active**
Are you a top?	**¿Eres activo?**
Are you a top or a bottom?	**¿Eres activo o pasivo?**
I am a 100% bottom.	**Soy pasivo ciento por ciento.**

166

I am a 100% top.	**Soy activo ciento por ciento.**
I am both, more active.	**Soy los dos, más activo.**
I am versatile.	**Soy versatile.**
I like top.	**Me gusta ser activo.**

(to) Touch   **tocar**

Touch me.	**¡Tócame!**
Don't touch me.	**No me toques.**
I want to touch you.	**Deseo tocarte.**
You want to touch it?	**¿Quieres tocarla?**
Come on. Touch it.	**¡Vamos! ¡Tócala!**
It is large/big.	**Es muy grande.**

U

(to be)Unfaithful   **ser infiel**
                               ponerle los cuernos

Are you faithful?	**¿Eres fiel?**
Yes, I am very faithful.	**Sí, soy muy fiel.**
José is unfaithful.	**José es infiel.**
	A José le pone los cuernos.
Don't be unfaithful.	**¡No seas infiel!**
	¡No le ponga los cuernos!
He was unfaithful.	**Él fue infiel.**
	A él le puso los cuernos.

I believe in fidelity.	Creo en fidelidad.
Be faithful!	¡Sé fiel! o ¡Sea fiel!
We believe in fidelity.	Creemos en fidelidad.

(to) Untie   **desatar**

| Untie me | ¡Desátame! |
| Don't untie me. | ¡No me desates! |

(to) Urinate   **orinar**

                 urinar

I have to urinate.	Tengo que orinar/urinar.
I had to urinate.	Tenía que orinar/urinar.
	Tuve que orinar/urinar.
Did you have to urinate?	¿Tenias que urinar/orinar?

| Did you have to urinate? | ¿Tuviste que urinar/orinar? |
| Don't urinate on me | ¡No urines en mí! |

I don't like water sports.

No me gustan deportes de agua.

V

Venerial Disease VD   **la Enfermedad**

    He has VD.   **Él tiene la enfermedad.**

    He has STDs.

Él tiene enfermedades sexuales.

Él tiene Enfermedades de Transmision Sexual (ETS)

    Be careful you guys.   **¡Tengan cuidado, amigos!**

Please, use condoms.

POR FAVOR. ¡USEN CONDONES!

Vibrator   **el vibrador**

    I need a good vibrator.   **Necesito un buen vibrador.**

    A vibrator without batteries.   **Un vibrador sin limas.**

    An electric vibrator.   **Un vibrador eléctico.**

With may speeds.

Con varias velocidades.

    The faster the better.

Lo mas rápido posible/mejor.

Vice   **un vicio**

I have a few vices in life.

Tengo unos pocos vicios de la vida.

I love to suck and fuck.   **Me encanta mamar y follar.**

They are not vices, they are necesities.

No son vicios, son necesidades.

Virgin   **virgen**

Are you virgin?   **¿Eres virgen?**

Yes, I am virgin.   **Sí, soy virgen.**

I have a virgin ass.   **Tengo culo virgen**

I am a virgin but I want you to change it. Fuck me!

Soy virgen y quiero que lo cambies. ¡Cójeme!

W

Well hung   **(bien) dotado**

                       (bien) vergudo

Is he hung?   **¿Es dotado?**

                            ¿Es vergudo

He is really hung.   **Él es bien dotado.**

                       Él es bien vergudo

Are you hung?   **¿Eres dotado?**

                            ¿ Eres vergudo?

Are you well hung?   **¿Eres bien dotado?**

Are you well hung?	**¿Eres bien vergudo?**
You are so hung.	**Eres tan dotado.**
	Eres tan vergudo.
You are hairy and hung.	**Eres peludo y vergudo.**
I am hung.	**Soy vergudo. Soy dotado.**
I am really hung.	**Soy muy dotado.**
	Soy muy vergudo.
I am not large.	**No soy grande.**

It not large but I know how to use it.

No es grande pero sé usarla.

Water sports	**deportes de agua.**
I like water sports.	**Me gustan deportes de agua.**
I don't like water sports.	**No me gustan deportes de agua.**
I like to piss in your mouth.	**Me gusta mear en tu boca.**
I like to shit in your face.	**Me gusta cagar en tu cara.**
Do you like water sports?	**¿Te gustan deportes de agua?**
No way. I don't like it.	**De ninguna manera, No me gustan.**
	Ni modo, No me gustan.

Whips   **látigos**

    I like whips and chains.   **Me gustan látigos y cadenas.**

    Leather and handcuffs   **La piel y esposas**

                           El cuero y esposas

    Suck and fuck   **Mamada y Follada**

General expressions

Greetings and Salutations

Including: numbers, colors, clothes, places in the city, the home, meeting people and etc.

Greetings and Salutions

Good morning	**Buenos días** o **Muy buenos**
Good afternoon	**Buenas tardes** o **Muy buenas**
Good evening/night	**Buenas noches** o **Muy buenas**

| Hello | **Hola** |
| Good bye | **Adiós** |

See you later	**Hasta Luego**
	Nos vemos
	Hasta la vista
	Chau

What is your name?	**¿Cómo te llamas?**
	¿Cuál es tu nombre?
My name is…	**Me llamo…**
	Mi nombre es…

How are you?	**¿Cómo estás?**
I am well, thank you.	**Estoy bien. Gracias.**
… and you?	**…¿y tú?**
I am tired.	**Estoy cansado.**
…sick/ill.	**…enfermo.**

...busy.	...ocupado.
Yes.	**Sí.**
No.	**No.**
Please.	**Por favor**
Thank you.	**Gracias.**
You are welcome.	**De nada.**
	Por nada. o No hay de que.

Questioning words	**Palabras Interrogativas**

Where?	**¿Dónde...?**
When?	**¿Cuándo...?**
How?	**¿Cómo...?**
Why?	**¿Por qué...?**
How much?	**¿Cuánto...?**
Who?	**¿Quién...?**
What?	**¿Qué...?**
What? (what did you say?)	**¿Cómo...?**
Which?	**¿Cuál/ cuáles(pl) ...?**
For what reason/purpose?	**¿Para qué...?**

What is your address?	**¿Cúal es tu dirección?**
My address is...	**Mi dirección es...**

Where do you live?		¿**Dónde vives?**	
I live at/in…		**Vivo en …**	
What is your telephone number?			
		¿**Cuál tu número de teléfono?**	
My number is…		**Mi número es…**	

NUMBERS   **Números**

One	**uno**	six	**seis**
Two	**dos**	seven	**siete**
Three	**tres**	eight	**ocho**
Four	**cuatro**	nine	**nueve**
Five	**cinco**	ten	**diez**

Eleven	**once**	sixteen	**diez y seis**
Twelve	**doce**	seventeen	**diez y siete**
Thirteen	**trece**	eighteen	**diez y ocho**
Fourteen	**catorce**	nineteen	**diez y nueve**
Fifteen	**quince**	twenty	**veinte**

176

NUMBERS (Cont.)   **Números**

From more than *twenty* you just add **Y** and the numbers from *1-9*

Twenty	**veinte**
Twenty one	**veinte y uno**
Twenty two	**veinte y dos**

Getting the picture? *Great*

Thirty	**treinta**
Thirty on	**treinta y uno**
Forty	**cuarenta**
Fifty	**cincuenta**
Sixty	**sesenta**
Seventy	**setenta**
Eighty	**ochenta**
Ninety	**noventa**
One hundred	**cien/ciento**

Numbers above one hundred are not too bad. Let's look!

100	**en/ciento**
101	**ciento uno**
102	**ciento dos**
110	**ciento diez**
120	**ciento veinte**
200	**dos cientos**
201	**dos cientos uno**

177

220	dos cientos veinte
221	dos cientos veinte y uno
300	tres cientos
400	cuatro cientos
500	*quinientos
501	quinientos uno
600	seis cientos
700	*setecientos

Numbers (Cont.) **NÚMEROS**

800	ocho cientos
900	*novecientos
1000	mil
1001	mil uno
1002	mil dos
2020	dos mil veinte

*Before a thousand put the other number in front of **mil***

3000	tres mil
5000	cinco mil
10.000	diez mil
30.000	treinta mil

Let's look at 1999 and 2006. I will break it down for you.

1000	**mil**
2000	**dos mil**
900	**novecientos**
2006	*dos mil seis*
1999	**mil novecientos noventa y nueve**

Enough of the numbers. OK?

Where are you from ?	**¿De dónde eres?**
I am from…	**Soy de…**
United States	**…Estados Unidos.**
Spain	**…España.**
México/Méjico.	**…México/Méjico.**
I am an American.	**Soy estadounidense.**
	Soy americano
…Spaniard.	**… español.**
…Mexican.	**…mexicano/mejicano.**
…Argentine.	**…argentino**
…Peruvian.	**…peruano.**

Colors	**los colores**
What color is the car?	¿De qué color es el coche?
It is red.	Es rojo
....blue.	...azul.
....yellow	...amarrillo.
....orange.	...anaranjado.
....black.	...negro.
....white.	...blanco.
....green.	...verde.
....brown.	...pardo.
	...color de café
	...moreno.
....pink.	...rosado.
...dark blue.	...azul oscuro.
...sky blue.	...azul celeste.

Clothes	**la ropa**
Do you have a shirt?	¿Tienes (la/una)camisa?
	...pants?
	...(los/unos)pantalones?

180

...short pants?

...(los/unos)pantalones cortos?

...socks?   ...caletines?

...shoes?   ...zapatos?

I have a shirt.   Tengo camisa.

...belt.   ...cinturón.

...t-shirt.   ...camiseta.

...t-shirt for the beach.   ...playera.

...underwear.   ...ropa interior.

...shorts.   ...calzones.

                               ...calzoncillos

...swim suit   ...traje de baño

...jock strap   ...sorporte atlético

...sun glasses.   ...gafas de sol.

THE HOUSE   **La Casa**

Living room	la sala
Dining room	el comedor
Bedroom	la habitación
	el dormitorio
	la recáma
Bedroom(Cont.)	la habitación
Bedroom	el cuarto de dormir
Bathroom	el baño
Hallway	el pasillo

Closet	**el closet**
	el armario
garage	**el garaje**
What's in each room?	**¿Qué hay en cada cuarto?**
Living room	**la sala**
Couch/sofa	**el sofá**
Arm chair	**el sillón**
Lamp	**la lámpara**
Tables	**las mesas**
Book case	**el estante para libros**
Telephone	**el teléfono**
Television	**el televisor/la televisión**
Stereo	**el esterio**
Bedroom	**la habitación**
Bed	**la cama**
Head board	**la cabecera**
Blanket	**la cobija/la manta**
Sheets	**las sábanas**
Pillow	**la almohada**
Mattress	**el colchón**
Bed table	**el tocador**
Carpet	**la alfombra**

Bathroom	**el baño**
Bathtub	**la bañera**
Shower	**la ducha**
Toilet	**el retrete**
What's in each room?	**¿Qué hay en cada cuarto?**
Bathroom(Cont.)	**el baño**
	el inodoro
	el excusado
Toilet seat	**el asiento del inodoro**
Towel	**la toalla**
Towel rake	**el toallero**
Sink	**el lavabo**
Facet	**el grifo**
Hot and cold water	**agua caliente y fría**
Toilet paper	**el papel higiénico**
	el papel de baño
	un rollo de papel
soap	**el jabón**
shower curtain	**la cortina de ducha**
Kitchen	**la cocina**
Stove	**la estufa**
Oven	**el orno**

Refrigeator	**el refrigeador**
	la nevera
	el frigorífico
Sink	**el fregadero**
Dishes	**los platos**
Glasses	**los vasos**
Cups	**las tazas**

Places to go	**Lugares para visitar/ir**
downtown	**el centro**
dain square	**la plaza mayor**
Movie theater	**el cine**
drt gallery	**la galería de arte**
theatre	**el teatro**
night club	**el cabaret**
	el club nocturo
	un disco
	una discoteca
bullfight	**la corrida de toros**
museum	**el museo**
church	**la iglesia**
sinague	**la singoga**
mosque	**la mesquita**

temple	**el templo**
beach	**la playa**
swimming pool	**la piscina**
	la alberca
department store	**el almacén**
shopping mall	**el centro de compras**
market	**el mercado**
supermarket	**el supermercado**
restaurant	**el restaurante**
coffee shot	**la cafetería**
	el café
bar	**el bar**
post office	**el correo**
city hall	**el ayuntamiento**
school	**la escuela**
college	**la universidad**
hospital	**el hospital**
clinic	**la clínca**
More places to go.	**Más lugares para visitar/ir**
doctor's	**el médico**
bus station	**la estación de autobuses**
subway	**el metro**
bus stop	**la parada del autobuses**
train station	**la estación de trenes**

airport	**el aeropuerto**
newspaper office	**la oficina de la prensa**
the country	**el campo**
ranch	**el rancho**
	la estancia
	la plantación
police station	**la estación de policía**
palace of fine arts	**el palacio de bellas artes**
ballet	**el ballet**
concert	**el concierto**

Gay Places to go.	**Lugares Gay**
baths	**los baños**
saunas	**las saunas**
prono movies	**las películas prono**
porno theater	**el cine prono**
gay beach	**la playa gay**
nude beach	**la playa nudista**
gay clubs	**clubes gay**
gay disco	**disco gay**
sex shop	**tienda gay**
sex shop	**un sex shop**
the gay area	**la zona gay**
gay neighborhood	**el barrio gay**

private club	**un club privado**
male whore house	**casa de putos**
house of boys	**casa de chicos**

Metric
Can be Fun!

How do you size up?

(size, weight, height, distance and weather)

METRIC   METRIC   METRIC

The USA does not use metric but, I have a guide
for you to make it easy to underdstand. **So how
big is big? Let's size up thing for you.**

How large/big are you?

¿Cuánto mides?
¿Cuántos centímetros tienes?

> I measure......
>> *Mido.....centímetros.*
>
> I have.....
>> *Tengo.....centímetros.*

Inches	Centímetros (cm.)
5	12.7 cm.
5½	13.97 cm.
6	*15.24 cm.*
*6 ½	16.51 cm.
7	17.78 cm.
**7 ½	19.05 cm.
8	**20.32 cm.**
***8 ½	**21.59 cm.**
9	**22.86 cm.**
9 ½	**24.13 cm.**
10	**25.40 cm.**

Anyone with 10 inches or more than 25.40 cm. is MUY GRANDE amigos!
In case, here are a few more. But, let's be real, nothing over a foot. Smile!
What a fantasy eh? WOW !

10 ½	**26.67 cm.**
11	**27.94 cm.**
11 ½	**29.21 cm.**
12	*30.48 cm.*
12 ½	*31.75 cm.*
13	*33.02 cm.*

Enough, that's more than I can handle! I have entered into the danger zone.

Weight   Weight   Weight

¿Cómo pesas?   How much do you weight?
Peso.......kilos. *(Todo depende de altura)*

Pounds	Kilogramas o Kilos
102	*46.27*
104	*47.17*
106	*48.17*
108	*48.08*
110	*49.90*
120	54.43
130	58.97
140	63.50
150	*68.04*
160	*72.57*
170	*77.1*
180	*81.65*
190	*86.18*
200	90.72
210	95.25
220	99.79

How tall are you?

¿Cuánto mides de altura?

I am .... Tall   *Mido..... metros.* (de altura)

Feet	Metros
5	1.52
(uno cincuenta y dos)	
5.1	1.55
5.2	1.58
Bajo/chaparro	
5.3	1.62
5.4	1.65
5.5	1.68
5.6	1.71
Bajito/Mediano	
5.7	1.74
5.8	*1.77*
5.9	*1.80*
5.10	*1.83*
Mediano	
5.11	*1.86*
Mediano/poco alto	
6	*1.89*

6.1	**1.92**
Alto	
6.2	**1.95**
6.3	1.98
6.4	2.01
6.5	2.04
Muy Alto	
6.6	2.07
6.7	2.10
6.8	2.13
6.9	2.16
Wow/Grande/Altísimo	
6.10	2.19
6.11	2.21
7	2.24
Grandísimo	

Miles and Miles to go. *Kilométros y Kilométros para viajar.*

1	1.61
5	8.05
10	16.09
15	24.14
20	32.19
25	40.23
30	48.28
35	56.33
40	64.37
50	80.47
60	96.56
70	112.65
80	128.75
90	144.84
100	160.93

How far is it? **¿A qué distancia?**

It is.... **Es.....kilométros.**

It is ... from here. ***Es..... kilométros de aquí.***

It is close, only ....
Está cerca, solamente unos..... kilométros.

It is far, only....
Está lejos, solamente unos.....   kilométros.

North   **el norte**

South   **el sur**

East   **el este**

West   **el oeste**

What's the weather like?

¿Qué tiempo hace?

It is warm.   **Hace calor.**
It is very warm/hot.   **Hace mucho**
calor.

It is cold.   **Hace frío.**
It is really cold   **Hace mucho**
frío.

It is chilly.   **Hace fresco.**
It is windy   **Hace viento.**

The sun is shining.
Hay sol/Hace sol.
        It is cloudy
        Está nublado
It is clear skys.   **Está despejado.**

It is going to rain.	Va a llover.
It's raining.	Llueve o Está lloviendo.
It is going to snow.	Va a nevar.
It is snowing	Nieva o Está nevando.

What is the temperature?
¿Cuál es la temperatura?
¿Qué temperatura es?

La temperaturs es........

Farenheit		Celsius
32		0.
34		1.11
36		2.22
38		3.33
	Frío	
40		4.44
50		10.00
	Fresco	
60		15.56
70		**21.11**
72		**22.22**

74	**23.45**
	Agradable/Cómodo
76	**24.45**
78	**25.56**
80	**26.67**
82	**27.78**
	Calor
84	**28.89**
86	**30.00**
88	**31.11**
90	**32.22**
	Mucho Calor/Caloroso
92	**33.34**
94	**34.45**
96	35.56
98	36.67
	Horrible/Terrible
100	37.78

Expressions
Of

LOVE

Terms
Of
Endearments

Expressions of Love:	**EXPRESIONES DE AMOR**
My love	**Mi amor.**
…light of my life	**Luz de mi vida.**
…heart of my life	**Corazón de mi vida.**
My dear/sweet heart	**Mi querido.**
My doll baby	**Mi muñeco.**
…little doll baby	**…muñequito.**
My forbidden love.	**Mi amor prohibido.**
My lover	**Mi amante.**
My partner	**Mi pareja.**
My sugar daddy	**Mi bomboncito.**
My special friend	**Mi amigo especial.**
My close friend	**Mi amigo íntimo.**
My dear friend	**Mi querido amigo.**
My sweet friend	**Mi dulce amigo.**
My affecionate friend	**Mi cariñoso amigo.**
My handsome friend	**Mi guapo amigo.**

My cute friend

Mi lindo amigo.

Mi bonito amigo.

Do you love me?

¿Me quieres?

¿Me amas?

Yes, I love you a lot.

Sí, te quiero mucho.

Sí, te amo mucho.

I really love you.
Te quiero de verdad.
Te amo de verdad.

I need you to fulfill/complete l my life.
Te necesito para cumplir mi vida.

My life is complete with you in it.
Mi vida está completa contigo.

I don't want anyone in my life but you.
No quiero a nadie en mi vida sino tú.

I cannot live without you.
No puedo vivir sin ti.

You are my whole world.
Eres mi mundo entero.

Never leave me.	**Nunca me dejes.**
	Nunca salgas de mí.
I will never cheat on you.	**Nunca te engaño.**
	No te engaño nunca.

We are very stable in our lifes.
Somos estables en nuestras vida.

You are my strength and fortress.
Eres mi fuerza y fortaleza.

I love you more than anything.
Te amo más que nada.
Te quiero más que nada.

We love each other more than anything.
Nos queremos más que nada.
Nos amamos más que nada.

More than anyone.	**Más que nadie.**

I want you with me always.
Te deseo conmigo por siempre.

You are so important to me.
Me eres tan importante.

You give me so much affection and love.
Me das tanto cariño y amor.

You are the soul of my being.
Eres el alma de mi ser.

You are the heart of my being.
Eres el corazón de mi ser.

I want to share my love only with you.
Sólo quiero compartir mi amor contigo.

Life and love is saring.
La vida y el amors son de compartir.

I will never abandon you.   **Nunca te abandono.**

I am here only for you, my love.
Sólo estoy aquí para ti, mi amor.

I show my love for you everyday.
Te muestro mi amor todos los días.

I enjoy being in your arms.
Gozo de estar entre tus brazos.

…wrapped in your arms.
…envueltos entre tus brazos.

I adore you so much.   **Te adoro tanto.**

I worship you a lot.   **Te alabo mucho**

You are my inspiration.   **Eres mi inspiración.**

I will never forget the life we have.
Nunca me olvido la vida que tenemos.

…our life as one.
…nuestra vida como una.

I need your hugs and kisses.

Necesito tus abrazos y besos.

Life is too short. **La vida es muy corta.**

Let's life life to the fullest. **Vamos a vivir la vida**
a la máxima.

Vivamos la vida a la
máxima.

Your life is my life. **Tu vida es mi vida.**

My life is your life. **Mi vida es tu vida.**

Our life is one. **Nuestra vida es una.**

I will love you forever. **Te quiero por**
siempre.

Te amo por siempre.

Love me with all your heart and soul.
Quiéreme con todo el corazón y alma.
Ámame con todo el corazón y alma.

I do love you with all my heart and soul.
Te quiero con todo mi corazón y alma.
Te amo con todo mi corazón y alma.

Life is beautiful. **La vida es bell**
A genuine love. **Un amor verdadero.**
Un amor genuíno.

Our love is complete.
Nuestro amor está completa.

I want to wake up with you everyday of my life.
Quiero amanecer contigo cada día de mi vida.

ABC's

Some Important
Descriptive Words
and
Their Usages

ABC's for descriptive words their usages.

a little   **un poco**

I speak Spanish a little.   **Hablo español, un poco.**

all the time   **todo el tiempoI**

I go to that bar all the time. **Voy a ese bar todo el tiempo.**

always   **siempre**

He is alway very nice   **Siempre él es muy simpático.**

angry   **enojado**

He is angry with me.   **Él está enojado conmigo.**

arrogant   **arrogante**

I don't like arrogant people.**No me gusta gente arrogante.**

attractive   **atractivo**

Wow, he is so attractive.   **Wow, él es tan atractivo.**

bad   **malo**

Don't be so bad.   **¡No seas tan malo!**

best   **el mejor**

He is the best of all.   **Él es el mejor de todos.**

better   **mejor**

So much the better.   **Tanto mejor.**

blond   **rubio**

I like blond guys.   **Me gustan los rubios**

boring   **aburrido**

I am bored, let's go out.   **Estoy aburrido, salgamos.**

bothered   **fastidiado**

Why are yo bothered?   **¿Por qué estás fastiado?**

brave   **valiente**

We are brave.   **Somos valientes**.

cheap   **barato**

The drinks are cheep.   **Las bebidas son baratos.**

clean   **limpio**

This place is clean.   **Este lugar está limpio.**

clear   **claro**

It is clear, we don't get along.   **Es claro que no nos**

llevamos bien.

content   **contento**

We are content/happy here.   **Estamos contentos aquí.**

courteous   **cortés**

He's not courteous.   **Él no es cortés**

cute   **bonito/lindo**

You are cute.   **Eres bonito/lindo.**

dark-skinned   **moreno**

They are dark skinned.   **Son morenos.**

delicious   **delicioso**

You are so delicous.   **Eres tan delicioso.**

depressed   **deprimido**

I am not depressed.   **No estoy deprimido.**

different   **diferente**

They are so differente.   **Ellos son tan diferentes.**

dirty   **sucio**

How dirty!   **¡Qué sucio!**

early   **temprano**

I will be there early.   **Voy a estar allí temprano.**

easy   **fácil**

It is easy to get to know me.   **Es fácil conocerme.**

elegant   **elegante**

You are so elegant tonight!   **¡Eres tan elegante esta noche!**

embarrassed   **avergonzado**

I am so embarrased that he used me.

Estoy avergonzado que él me usó.

every day   **todos los días**

Everyday we make love.   **Todos los días hacemos el amor.**

excellent   **excelente**

An excellent opportunity.   **Una oportunidad excelente.**

expensive   **car**

He sales his body and it is expensive.

Él se vende su cuerpo y está/es caro.

faithful   **fiel**

    My boyfriend is faithful.   **Mi novio es fiel.**

famous   **famoso**

    This is a famous place. **Éste es un lugar famoso.**

far   **lejos**

    Is it far?   **¿Está lejos?**

fat   **gordo**

    I don't like fat guys. **No me gustan tíos gordos.**

first   **primer/o/a**

    It was my first time. **Fue mi primera vez.**

foolish   **tonto**

    How foolish! **¡Qué tonto!**

from time to time   **de vez en cuando**

From time to time we go dancing.

De vez en cuando vamos a bailar.

fun   **divertido**

I like being with you because your are so fun.

Me gusta estar contigo porque eres tan divertido.

good   **bueno**

Was it good?   **¿Estuvo bueno?**

good-looking   **guapo**

You are really good looking and sexy.

Eres muy guapo y sexy.

great   **genial**

How great!   **¡Qué genial!**

happy   **alegre/feliz**

We were happy together.

Éramos alegres/Estábamos felices .

happy	contento
We are very happy.	**Estamos contentos.**

hardly	apenas
He hardly ever speaks to strangers.	
Apenas habla con extranjeros.	

here	aquí
It is this way.	**Es por aquí.**

here	acá
I am here now.	**Ahora, estoy acá.**

hot	caliente
The food is hot.	**La comida está caliente.**

You are hot, daddy.	**Eres caliente, papi.**
I am horny for you .	**Estoy caliente por ti.**

important	importante
Why is it important?	**¿Por qué es importante?**

intelligent   **inteligente**

He's good looking and intelligent.

Él es guapo e inteligente.

kind   **simpático**

You are very kind my love.

Eres muy simpático, mi amor.

larger/bigger   **más grande**

Your penis is larger than José's.

Tu pene es más grande que el de José.

largest/biggest   **el más grande**

Your cock is the largest I have seen.

Tu polla es la más grande que he visto.

You have the largest cock of all.

Tienes la polla más grande de todas.

last Monday   **el lunes pasado**

Last Monday, I met the love of my life

El lunes pasado conocí/encontré el amor de mi vida.

last night   **anoche**

Last night, we had sex.   **Anoche, tuvimos sexo.**

last week   **la semana pasada**

Last week we went to a gay disco.

La semana fuimos a un disco gay.

last year   **el año pasado**

Last year was our anniversary.

El año pasado fue nuestro aniversario

late   **tarde**

Why are you late?   **¿Por qué estás tarde?**

lazy   **perezoso**

They are really lazy.   **Ellos son muy perezosos.**

large/big   **grande**

Are you big?   **¿Estás grande?**

many times   **muchas veces**

We fuck many times a day.

Follamos muchas veces al día

Mature	**maduro**
I like mature men.	**Me gustan hombres maduros.**
near	**cerca**
It is near/close.	**Está cerca.**
neither	**tampoco**
Me neither.	**Ni yo tampoco.**
never	**nunca**
I never have sex on the first date.	
Nunca tengo sexo en la primera cita.	
new	**nuevo**
A new boyfriend?	**¿Un novio nuevo?**
newly	**recién**
newly acquainted	**Recién conocido.**
nice/loveable	**amable**
You are so kind/sweet/loveable.	**Eres muy amable.**
now	ahora
Now they are a couple.	**Ahora es una pareja.**

of course	**por supuesto/claro/claro que**
sí/cómo no	

Of course, I love you .**Por supuesto, te quiero.**

Sí, cómo no, te quiero.

Claro que sí, te amo

often	**a menudo**

I see you often at the disco.

Te veo a menudo en el disco.

old	**viejo**
He is very old.	**Él es muy viejo.**

older	**mayor**
I am older than you.	**Soy mayor que tú.**

oldest	**el mayor**
He is the oldest guy here.	**Él es el tío mayor acá.**

pleasant	**agradable**
How pleasant!	**¡Qué agradable!**

poor	**pobre**
Poor people.	**Gente pobre.**

proud	**orgulloso**
I am very proud of you baby.	
Estoy muy orgulloso de ti mi amor.	

prepared	**preparado**
Is it prepared?	**¿Está preparado?**
It is ready now.	**Está preparado ahora.**

quickly	**rápido**
Quickly, let's go.	
	Rápido, Vamos.

ready	**listo**
Are you ready?	**¿Estás listo?**
Yes, I am ready.	**Sí, estoy listo.**
He is very clever.	**Él es muy listo.**

realistic	**realista**
I used to be realistic.	**Yo era realista.**

right now	ahora mismo

Are you cuming right now?

¿Vienes ahora mismo?

¿Acabas ahora mismo?

¿Te corres ahora mismo?

romantic	romántico

I am a romantic. **Soy romántico.**

sad	triste

Why are you sad baby?

¿Por qué estás triste mi amor?

selfish	egoísta

I don't like him, he is very selfish.

No me cae bien, es muy egoísta.

serious	serio

I am serious. **Estoy en serio.**

short	bajo

He is very short. **Él es muy bajo.**

He has a short/small cock. **Él tiene polla pequeña**

Él tiene verga pequeña.

Él tiene pene pequeño

shy	**tímido**
He used to be shy.	**Él era tímido.**

side	**lado**
He is next to me.	**Él está al lado de mí**

slowly	**despacio/lento**
Speak slowly, please.	**¡Hable despacio, por favor!**
He speaks slowly.	**Él habla lentamente.**

small **pequeño**

Man, his dick is small.

Hombre, la polla de él es pequeña.

smaller **más pequeño**

Su verga es más pequeña que la mía.

smallest **el más pequeño**

The smallest cock in the world.

La pinga más pequeña del mundo.

so much	**tanto**
I love you much.	**Te quiero tanto.**

sociable	**sociable**
We are very sociable.	**Somos muy sociables.**

sometimes	**algunas veces/a veces**
Sometimes he never comes home.	
Algunas veces no regresa nunca a casa.	

soon	**pronto**
See you soon.	**Hasta pronto.**

still/yet	**todavía**
I still love you .	**Todavía te quiero.**

strong	**fuerte**
He is muscular and strong.	
Él es musculoso y fuerte.	

suddenly	**de repente**
Suddenly, he kissed me.	**De repente, me besó.**

surprised   **sorprendido**

    I was so surprised to see you.

    Estuve tan sorprendido de verte.

tall   **alto**

    I love tall and sexy men.

    Me gustan hombres altos y sexy.

there   **allí**

    It's that way.   **Está por allí.**

there   **allá**(far away)

    It's way over there. **Está allá.**

thin   **delgado**

    I like slinder guys. **Me gustan hombres delgados.**

    He is very skinny. **Él es muy flaco.**

today   **hoy**

    Today is my birthday. **Hoy es mi cumpleaños.**

too much	demasiado
He fucks too much.	**Él folla demasiado.**
He pays too much for sex.	
Él paga demasiado por el sexo.	

too/also	**también**
Me too.	**Yo también**
	A mí tambié

ugly	**feo**
He is really ugly but has a big cock.	
Él es muy feo pero tiene una pinga muy grande.	

unbearable	**insoportable**
It is unbearable.	**Es insoportable.**

unhappy	**infeliz**
They have an unhappy relationshipe.	
Tienen una relación infeliz.	

weak	**débil**
I am not easy.	**No soy fácil.**

wise   **sabio**

    You are a wise man baby.

    Eres hombre sabio, mi amor.

without a doubt   **sin duda**

    Without a doubt, I desire you. Now.

    Sin duda, te deseo. Ahora.

worse   **peor**

    It is worse now.   **Es peor ahora.**

worst   **el peor**

    You are the worst guy in the world.

    Eres el hombre peor del mundo.

yesterday   **ayer**

    Yesterday, he fucked your brother.

    Ayer, cogió a su hermano.

    Ayer, folló a su hermano.

    Yesterday, he had sex with your brother.

    Ayer, tuvo sexo con su hermano.

young   **joven**

     I like young guys.   **Me gustan los jóvenes.**

     You are so/too young.   **Eres tan joven.**

                             Eres demasiado joven.

younger   **menor**

     You are younger than I am.

     Eres menor que yo.

     Do you like the younger guys?

     ¿Te gustan los menores?

youngest   **el menor**

     He is the youngest is the bar.

     Él es el menor del bar.

General Phrases. Enough!

Frases generales. Basta.

Let's get a Man.

Vamos a conseguir un Hombre.

Erotic Situations

from the Start to the Finish !

Una Fantasía

(to go) Cruising	**Ir de ligue.**
	Hacer la carrera
(to) Look for a Man.	**Buscar un hombre.**
Let's go crusing.	**Vamos de ligue.**
	¡Hagamos la carrera!
	Vamos a buscar hombres.
	¡Busquemos hombres!
Do you want to go cruising?	**¿Quieres ir de ligue?**
	¿Quieres hacer la
carrera?	
	¿Quieres buscar
hombres?	
Let's look for horny men.	**¡Busquemos a**
hombres calientes!	
	¡Busquemos a
hombres vellludos!	
	¡Busquemos a
hombres cachondos!	
	Vamos a buscar
hombres calientes.	
He is hot.	**Él es caliente.**

I like hairy men.

Me gustan hombres peludos.

Me gustan hombres velludos.

I like hairy chested men.

Me gustan hombres con vellos en el pecho.

I like hung men.

Me gustan hombres bien dotados.

I like hung men.

Me gustan hombres bien vergudos.

I like hung men.

Me gustan hombres con pollas grandes.

I like hung men.

Me gustan hombres con pingas grandes.

He is hairy.	**Él es velludo.**
He is hairy.	**Él es peludo.**
He is really hairy.	**Él es muy peludo.**
He is very hung.	**Él es bien dotado.**
He is very hung.	**Él es muy vergudo.**
Are you hairy?	**¿Eres peludo?**
Are you hung?	**¿Estás/Eres dotado?**

Do you have a big cock?	¿Tienes polla grande?
	¿Tienes pinga grande?
	¿Tienes verga grande?
I have a big cock.	Tengo polla grande.
	Tengo rábano grande.
	Tengo verga grande.
Show it to me.	¡Muéstramela!
Damn, That is big.	Ay, Carajo, ¡Qué
grande!	
Man, that is a nice cock.	Hombre, qué rica (es
tu polla.)	
You have a nice cock.	Tienes buena polla.
	Tienes buena pinga.
	Tienes buena verga.

Do you want to suck my cock?

¿Quieres mamard mi verga/polla/pinga?

Oh, baby, let me suck your big cock.

Oh, papi. Déjame mamar tu polla grande.

I want to suck it.	**Quiero mamártela.**

Do you like to suck big cocks?

¿Te gusta mamar pingas grandes?   ¿

Te gusta chupar pollas grandes?

Of course, I like big dicks.

Sí, por supuesto. Me gustan mamar pollas grandes.

Suck it.	**¡Mámala!**
	¡Chúpala!
Suck me off.	**¡Mámamela!**
Make that cock hard.	**Ponte dura esa polla**
	Hazla dura esa pinga.
Make that cock hard.	**¡Páratela!**
Make me hard. Suck it.	**…¡Que te me pongas**
tiesa! ¡Mámala!	
You make me hard.	**Se me pone dura.**
You suck it good, baby.	**La mamas muy bien,**
papi.	
I am going to cum.	**Me voy a correr.**
	Voy a venir.
	Voy a acabar.
Did you cum?	**¿Te corriste?**
	¿Viniste?
	¿Acabaste?
I want to cum in your mouth.	**Quiero acabar en tu boca.**
	Quiero venir en tu boca.
I came.	**Me corrí.**
	Vine.
	Acabé

I want your cum.	Quiero tu leche.
Do you want it?	¿La quieres?
Cum, baby, cum!	¡Córrete, papi, córrete!
Suck me till I cum.	¡Mámame hasta que
me venga!	
	¡Mámame hasta que me corra!
	¡Mámame hasta que me acabe!
I want all your cum.	Quiero tada tu leche.
Cum inside me baby.	¡Córreteme dentro papi!
Don't cum inside me.	¡No me te corras dentro de mí!
Take it out before you cum.	¡Sácala antes de acabar!
I am cuming again.	Me estoy corriendo de
nuevo.	
	Me corro otra vez.
	Vengo de nuevo.
Have you cum?	¿Te has corrido? (¿Te
corriste)	
	¿Has venido?
(¿Viniste?)	
Cum on my chest.	¡Córrete sobre mi
pecho!	
	…¡que vengas sobre
mi pecho!	
I really like it.	Me encanta mucho.

It taste really good, baby.

Me apetece el sabor de tu leche.

Que rica, baby. Mmmmmmm

You are making me hot.	**Me pones caliente.**
	Me estás poniendo caliente.
You are driving me crazy/wild.	
Me estás volviendo loco.	
	Me vuelves loco.
You like it, don't you?	
¿Te gusta? ¿Sí? o ¿Verdad?	

Oh, baby, I love it. Don't stop.	**Ah, papi me encanta**
mucho. ¡No Pares!	

You have a nice ass.	**Tienes un culo bonito.**
....sweet	**Tienes un culo dulce.**
....delicious.	**...delicioso.**
....tight.	**...apretado.**
....hairy.	**...velludo.**
Do you like to fuck?	**¿Te gusta follar?**
	¿Te gusta coger?
Yes, I love to fuck.	**Sí, me gusta follar/coger.**

Would you like to fuck me?	¿Te gustaría follarme?
	¿Te gustaría cogerme?
I would lvoe to fuck you.	Me gustaría cogerte.
	Me gustaría follarte.
I want your hard cock up my ass.	Quiero esa polla dura
en mi culo.	
You want it?	¿La quieres?
Yes, I want it a lot.	Sí, la quiero mucho.
Put it me and don't take it out.	¡Métemela y no la
saques!	
Man, you are so hot!	¡Hombre, eres tan
caliente!	
Fuck me!	¡Fóllame!
Fuck me hard.	¡Cójeme fuerte!
Harder.	Más fuerte.
Deep.	Al fondo.
Deeper.	Más al fondo
I am going in slowly.	Voy a entrar despacio, muy suave.

I am going in slowly.

Voy a metértela despacio, muy suave.

Then, I am going to ram it in.

Entonces, te la voy a clavar.

Entonces, voy a clavártela.

Ram it in, baby.   **¡Clávamela! Papi.**

I am going to fuck you so hard.

Voy a follarte a lo duro.

Te voy a follar a lo bruto.

Go in nice and slow and then harder.

¡Penétrame muy suave, y entonces muy fuerte!

Be gentle at first.   **¡Sé suave al principio!**

                                         ¡Sé suave al inicio!

Then, fuck me hard.

Entonces ¡cógeme muy fuerte!

Don't be easy, fuck me hard.

¡No seas suave, fóllame muy fuerte!

Take it out and ram it in again.

¡Sácala y clávamela de nuevo!

Go on, don't stop!
¡Sigue y no pares nunca!

Can I cum in your ass?   **¿Puedo venir en tu culo?**

                                Puedo correrme en tu culo?

                                ¿Puedo acabar en tu culo?

I want to cum in your hot ass.
Quiero correrme en tu culo caliente.
Quiero acabar en tu culo caliente.

I want to fill youd ass with my cum of love and passion.
Quiero llenar tu culo con la leche de mi amor y pasión

Now, Sit on my big hot cock   and let's do it again
Ahora, siéntate en mi grande polla caliente y follamos otra vez.

Did you like it?   **¿Te gustó?**

I like it a lot.   **Me gustó mucho.**

You really know how to fuck.
Sabes follar muy bien. Pero muy bien.

Thank you baby.   **Gracias. Papi.**

234

Do you want to take a shower? **¿Quieres bañarnos?**

Sure. And do you know, I want to fuck you in the shower.
Sí, y sabes que quiero follarte en la ducha.

I would love to give you a blow job in the shower.
Me gustaría darte una mamada en la ducha.

Let's shower! **Vamos a bañarnos.**
¡Bañémonos!

I have never had sex in the shower.
No he hecho nunca el sexo en la ducha.

I have never made love in the shower.
No he hecho nunca el amor en la ducha.

I have never fucked in the shower.
No he follado nunca en la ducha.

I like have sex in the shower.
Me gusta tener sexo en la ducha.

After we shower, do you want to do it again.

Después de bañarnos, ¿Quieres hacerlo de nuevo?

Man, you are a sex animal.
Hombre, eres un animal de sexo.

I am a sex animal of the night.
Soy animal de sexo de noche.

OK, Let's do it!
Bueno, Vamos.

Oh, by the way, you have a great body.
A próposito, tienes un cuerpo magnífico.

I like your sexy body.
Me encanta tu cuerpo sexy

Very muscular.   **Muy muscular.**

                                      Muy musculoso.

Muscular, handsome, and hung.
Musculoso, guapo y bien dotado.

I want to kiss you all over.
Quiero besar todo tu cuerpo.

You can kiss me wherever.

Puedes besarme dondequieras.

I am going to kiss you from top to bottom.

Voy a besarte desde la cabeza hasta el pie.

Sucking your nipples and rimming your ass.

Chupando tu pezones y lamiéndote tu culo.

I am in your hands. Do what you want baby.

Estoy en tus manos. Haz lo que quieras.

I am under your spell.

Estoy bajo de tu encanto.

I am under your control.

Estoy bajo de tu control.

What a dream!

¡Qué sueño!

What a fantasy!

¡Que fantasia!

ABC's

Spanish
to
English

Profanity
and
Colorful Expressions

Just getting DIRTY!

ABC's
Spanish to English
Getting a little Dirty.

A

A cuatro patas	doggie style
A la chingada	fuck it!/go to hell
A la verga	fuck it!
A la gran puta	oh, fuck it
Ah mierda	oh, shit!
A la mierda	go to hell!
Abadesa	pimp
Acabar	to cum/have orgasm
Acariciar	to caress/cuddle
Acariciarse	to fondle oneself/to masturbate
Afeminado	effeminate man
Agarrado	tightwad/stingy
Alzado	snob/stuck up
Amaricado	homosexual/gay
Amaricarse	to become a homosexual
Amante	lover
Amor	love

Amor a la primera vista	love at first sight
Ano	ass/anus/asshole
Atar	to tie/to tie up

B

Bastardo	bastard
Besar	to kiss
Beso	kiss
Beso francés	French kiss
Beso negro	the black kiss/rimming

B

(Cont.)

Bésame	kiss me
Besa mi culo	kiss my ass
Busequear	to smoother with kisses
Bicho	dick/cock/penis/pud
Bolas	balls
Bufa	fart
Bufetada	a slap
Bufo	fag/homosexual
Buscón	street walker/ one who looks for…

C

Cabrón	bastard/shitass
Cachar	to have sex/to ball
Cagar	to shit
Cagada	shit
Cagadero	shithouse/shitty place
está **Cagado**	you/he is full of shit
Calentar(ie)	to get hot/honry
Caliente	hot/horny
estar **Caliente**	to be horny/to be hot
Calientapollas	prick/cock teaser
Callejero	streetwalker
Caricia	caress
Cara de mierda	shit face
Cara de verga/polla	dick face
Cara de culo	ass face
Carajo	damn/fuck
...*vete* **al Carajo**	go to hell/go get fucked
Casa de putos	male whore house
Casas de niños	house of the 'boys'
Castrar	to castrate

241

Capullo	foreskin/a real dick/asshole
Clavar	to pound/hammer/nail/fuck
Cochón	fag/homo
Coger	to fuck/catch/seize or catch
Coger una mierda	to get fuck up/shit faced
Cogienda	fucking(the act of)
Cogetudo	an easy fuck
la Concha de tu madre	Your mother's cunt
Comer	to eat/to eat out someone
Coño	fuck/shit/ cunt/dumb ass/ etc.
¡qué Coño!	What a fucker/shit ass/ass hole etc.
Cojones	balls
…No tienes los Cojones	…You don't have the balls.
Colgantes	things that hang, balls
Cortejo	pimp/ escort
Crema	cream/semen
'cuarenta y uno'	un married at 41, homosexual
¡qué Cuero!	What a hunk!
Correrse	to cum/have orgasm
Chapete	easy fuck
Chapero	hustler
Chaquetear	to beat off/masturbate
Chavo bueno	handsome dude/hunk
Chinga tu madre	Mother fucker

Chingado	fuck/fucker
Chingao	fuck/fucker

Chingar	to fuck
Chupar	to suck
Chúpamela	suck me off
Chorizo	prick/sausage/dick
Churro	turd
Culo	ass
Culito	little ass/small
Culón	big ass
Curvas	curves

D

Dar mamada	to give a blowjob

E

Empalmarse	to get hard/to have a hardon
… se me empalmó	I got a hard on.
Enamorarse de	to fall in love with someone
…Me enamoro de ti.	I am falling in love with you.
Es pura paja.	That's shit.

Está a la verga. He is dicked face(drunk)

Estoy como gran puta. I am really like a great bitch/really pissed off.

Estoy jodido. I am really fucked/screwed.

F

por favor	please
el favor	...the pleasure of being fucked
follar	to fuck

G

Goma	rubber/condom

H

Hacer el amor	to make love
Hacer mierda	to fuck up/screw up
Hijo de gran puta	son of the great bitch
Hijo de puta	son of bitch
Hijo de una chingada madre	son of a fucking mother
Hideputa	son of bitch
Hijoputa	son of a bitch
Hijo de la chingada	son of the fucking bitch

Huevón	stupid/lazy/good for nothing/large balls
Huevos	balls/ nuts/ testicles

J

Joder	to fuck/Fuck
No me jodas	Don't fuck with me,
Estoy jodido	I'm fucked/screwed
Jodienda	paing in the ass/fucker
Jodontón	horny/fucking ready

L

Lameculos	ass licker
Leche	semen/cum/milk
... Tengo mala leche.	...I am in a bad mood
...un tío de mala leche.	. a bad mother fucker
Leche caliente	hot cum
Leche dulce	sweet cum
Leche amarga	bitter cum
Leche salada	salty cum
Llenar de mierda	to be full of shit

M

Madre	mother
..tu madre	you mother/fuck your mother
Madre de la chingada	mother of the fucker/mother

fucker

Mamada	blowjob
Mamar	to suck/give a BJ/to give head
Mamársela	to suck off
Mango	dick/cock
Marica	fag/homosexual
Maricón	fag/sissy/homosexual
Mariposa	fag/homosexul
Mear	to piss
Meada	a piss
Menear	to shake your ass
Menearse	to shake your cock/dick/masturbate

..Me meneo tres veces al día. I beat off 3 times a day.

Mierda	shit
Ni mierda	no shit
Minga	dick/cock

N

Nabo	dick/cock/prick

O

Ojete	asshole/anus
Ojo del culo	anus /asshole

P

Padrote	pimp
Paja	cock/dick/penis
Palo	cock/dick/penis
pararse	to have a hard on
Se le paró bien dura.	He got a big hard on.
estar **Parado**	to be hard
...Estoy parada.	I am hard.
Papi	daddy/baby/honey
Papi chulo	"sugar daddy"/cute daddy
Puta	bitch
Putear	to be whoring
...Vamos a Putear.	Let's go whoring
Putón	big male whore/stud

Pedo	fart
...estar **Pedo**	to be drunk
...está bien Pedo.	..he's really drunk
...hacer pedos	...to fart
Pelotas	balls
Pene	penis
Pendejo	stupid person/bastard/ SOB/pubic hair
Pico	dick/cock
Picha	dick/cock

P

(Cont.)

Pichar	to screw/fuck
Pija	dick/cock
Pinche	fucking/damned
...Pinche puto	...fucking male whore/bitch
Pinga	dick/ cock
Pingo	male whore
Pingón	male whore
Pito	dick/ cock
Polvo	screwing
echar un Polvo	to screw/ fuck
...Te echo un polvo.	...I fuck you
Polla	dick/cock
Ponerse dura	to get a hard on

248

…se me pone dura.	I got a hard on
Porra	dick/cock
Puñeta	beating off/masturbation
…*hacer* Puñeta	to beat off
…*hice* Puñeta.	I beat off.
Puto	male whore/fag/queer
***Ir de* Putos**	to go whoring
…Voy de **putos**	…I am going whoring.

R

Rábano   dick/cock

S

Serote   piece of shit

…pinche Serote …a fucking piece of shit

T

Tragar   to swallow

U

V

Verga   dick/cock

W

X

Y

Z

Zanahoria   cock/dick

The
Spanish World

with
Gay and Gay
Friendly
Destinations

Travel Adventures to Spanish Speaking Countries

The Spanish Speaking Countries opens up wonderful and exciting experiences. It is important that you research the country or countries that you are visiting. **Today, one of the best sources is the <u>World Wide Web</u>**. As I mentioned, I suggest to *Google.* An excellent search resource. **Respecting the cultural differences, customs and tradictions are important as a traveler. Remember that when you leave the United States, that you sacrifice many rights and privilegies and must adhere to a different country and to their laws. Be an intelligent traveler. Don't risk your travel by getting involved with the use of illigal drugs, it's not worth the time in jail.** *Again, do your homework. Have some understanding of the governments and mores of the vast Spanish Speaking Countries.*

Many are at the forefront of Gay and Human rights, where as others a making advancements more slowly. The larger cities and resorts may be more open than the rural areas and indigenous areas. The govenments and religious institutions have much control in the various communities. Public display of ones gayness could draw unwanted attention.

Below, I have listed the countries that are excellent and moving forward, and others there still may be more taboos. An * indicates very gay friendly.

Always practice SAFE SEX. And, be aware of 'gay for pay."

www.gaywire.net/newswire#677AAE

zoom.gay.com/home.webloc

www.planetoutinc.com/.webloc

www.gay.com/news/.webloc

www.purpleroofs.com.webloc   This is an excellent site for every country!

gayguide.net 1.webloc   Another   excellent site for every country!

España

Full rights for GLBT as well as marriage/partnerships

More than gay friendly cities. Experience Gay Spain.

*Madrid

*Barcelona

*Sitges

*Ibiza

*Benidorm

*Marbella

*Valencia

*Málaga

•Torremolinos

*Santander

*Bilbao

*Sevilla

*Granada

www.purpleroofs.com.webloc

gayguide.net 1.webloc

http://europeforvisitors.com/europe/articles/madrid_gay_lesbian.htm

http://www.gayiberia.com/

http://travel.gaycrawler.com/chronicles/ibiza.html

México

There is an openness in the large metropolitan areas of México. Some cities are more acepting that others. But you can have a great gay experience. Always be careful. Experience gay Mexico. You can get married in Mexico City and Saltillo.

*Mexico City(la Zona Rosa, Polanco, Centro Historico)

*Guadalajara

*Saltillo

*Ajijic(retirement area near Guadalajara)

*Puerto Vallarta(gay mecca)

*Cuernavaca

*Puebla

*Monterrey

*Oaxaca

•Mazatlán

*Mérida

*Veracruz

*Cancun

*Juchilán(in the State of Oaxaca)

www.purpleroofs.com.webloc

www.donpato.com/city.htm#67779D

http://www.donpato.com/aca.html

http://www.gaymexico.net/gdl.html

Guatemala

*Guatemala City (with caution but there is an ok gay scene)
Antigua (relaxing gay scene)
Panajachel (Lake Atitlán Area) (age of aquarius gay scene)

www.purpleroofs.com.webloc

gayguide.net 1.webloc

www.gayguatemala.com/.webloc

El Savador

San Salvador (the little gay scene is getting better)

www.purpleroofs.com.webloc

gayguide.net 1.webloc

www.gayelsalvador.com/.webloc

Nicaragua

Managua (the little gay scene is getting better)

www.purpleroofs.com.webloc

gayguide.net 1.webloc

prideslide.com/directory#6777D4

256

Honduras
Teguicigalpa (slow moving gay scene)

www.purpleroofs.com.webloc

gayguide.net 1.webloc

Costa Rica
*San José (Very nice gay scene)
*Miguel Antonio National Park on the Pacific

www.purpleroofs.com.webloc

www.gaycostarica.com/gui#6777E9

http://members.aol.com/GayCRica/guide.html

Panamá
Panamá City (gay scene but with caution)

www.purpleroofs.com.webloc

http://www.globalgayz.com/g-panama.html

gayguide.net 1.webloc

Colombia(

*Bogatá (gay scene getting better)
*Barranquilla(good gay scene)
*Cartagena
Medellín

gayguide.net 1.webloc

www.purpleroofs.com.webloc

poorbuthappy.com/colombi#67786A

Venezuela

*Caracas (good gay scene with caution)
Marcaribo

www.about-venezuela.com/.webloc
http://board.totalvenezuela.com/Gay
http://www.missvenezuelagay.com/
www.personalsguide.net/.webloc

el Ecuador

*Quito (good gay scene)
*Guayaquil

www.gayecuador.com/.webloc

www.quitogay.net/.webloc

www.purpleroofs.com.webloc

El Perú
   *Lima (colonial Lima,many hustlers)
   •*Miraflores*(upscale area of Lima, very good gay scene)
   *Arequipa(good scene)
   *Cusco
   *Trujillo

www.peruesgay.com/.webloc

www.gayperu.com/.webloc

www.purpleroofs.com.webloc

gayguide.net 1.webloc

Chile
   *Santiago (on the move, Very Good Gay scene)
   *Viña del Mar
   *Concepción
   *Valparaíso

www.purpleroofs.com.webloc

gaysantiagocl.tripod.com#6778C4

www.gaychile.com/index.p#6778C2

gayguide.net 1.webloc

Bolivia
La Paz (getting better slowly)
Santa Cruz
Cachabamba
Sucre

www.boliviagay.com/modul#6778D4

gayguide.net1.webloc

www.purpleroofs.com.webloc

la Argentina
First country in Latino America to grant legal partnerships/marriage.
*Buenos Aires(the Big Apple/Paris of South America)
La Recoleta (one of many outstanding areas of BsAs)
*Mar del Plata
*Mendoza
*Rosario
*Córdoba

www.thegayguide.com.ar/.webloc

http://www.gayscape.com/arg.html

http://www.gayjourney.com/hotels/argentina.htm

http://www.argentinagay.net/

Paraguay
Asunsión
gayguide.net 1.webloc

www.purpleroofs.com.webloc

www.globalgayz.com/g-par#6778EF

Uruguay
*Montevideo (good gay scene)

gayguide.net 1.webloc

www.purpleroofs.com.webloc

gayjourney.com/hotels/ur#6778FD

Puero Rico
*San Juan(Very good gay scene)
*Ponce
Bayamón

gayguide.net 1.webloc

www.purpleroofs.com.webloc

http://www.geocities.com/WestHollywood/9275/index-old.html

la República Dominicana
*Santo Domingo(active gay scene)

gayguide.net 1.webloc

www.purpleroofs.com.webloc

http://www.globalgayz.com/g-dominicanrepublic.html

Cuba
*la Habana(Very good gay scene, but be careful)

gayguide.net 1.webloc

www.purpleroofs.com.webloc

www.gay-cuba.com/.webloc

Travel Sites And Embassy Info

DirectorioHispano

España and Latino América
Argentina
Buenos
U.S. Embassy
Consular Section #4300
Columbia #1425
1-777-4533-45344525
Mailing Address: Unit 4334, APO AA 34034

Bolivia
la Paz
U.S Embassy
Consular Section Banco Popular del Perú Building
Corner of Calles Mercado and Colón
P.O.Box 425, *la Paz*
1-591-2-350-251
Mailing Address: APO AA 34032

Chile
Santiago

U.S. Embassy
Consular Section Codina
Building
Agustinas #1343
1-56-2-671-0133
Mailing Address: Unit 4127,
APO AA 34033

Costa Rica
San José

U.S. Embassy
Consular Post Pavas
1-506-20-2305
Mailing Address: APO
AA34020

Columbia
Bogotá

U.S. Embassy
Consular Section Calle#38
No. 8-61
Apartado Aereo #3831
1-57-1-228-5687
Mailing Address: APO AA
34038

Cuba
la Havana

U.S. Interest Section, Swiss
Embassy
Calzada entre L y M Vedado
Havana
Mailing Address: Dept. of
State
Washington, DC 20521-3200

El Salvador
San Salvador

U.S. Embassy
Consular Section Final Blvd.
Station Antigua Cuscatlan
1-503-78-6011
Mailing Address: Unit 3116
APO AA 34023

Ecuador
Quito

U.S. Embassy
Consular Section Avenida 12
de Octubre y   Avenida
Patria P.O. 538
1-593-2-502-052
Mailing Address: Unit 5309
APO AA 34039-3420
Consulate General-
Guayaquil-1-593-4-323-370

España
Madrid

U.S. Embassy
Consular Secton Serrano #75
28006
1-34-157-7400
Mailing Address: APO AE
09642

Honduras
Tegucigalp

U.S. Embassy
Consular Section Avenida La
Paz
1-50432-3120
Mailing Address: AMEMB
APO AA 34022

México
la Ciudad de México, DF

U.S. Embassy
Paseo de la Reforma
#30506500
1-52-5-211-0042
Mailing Address: P.O. Box
3087
Laredo, TX 78044-3087

México (Cont.)

Consulate General Offices

Ciudad Juarez   1-52-5-511-9980

Guadalajara   1-52-16-16-9056

Hermosillo   1-52-3-626-6549

Matamoros   1-52-17-2375

Mérid   1-52-99-25-5011

Monterrey   1-52-83-45-2120

Nicaragua
Managua

U.S. Embassy
Consular Section Km. 4-1/2
Carretera Sur
1-505-2-66-6010
Mailing Address: APOAA
34021

Paraguay
Asunción

U.S. Embassy
Consular Section 1776
Mariscal Lopez Ave.
1-595-21-213-715
Mailing Address: Unit 4711
APO AA 34036-00001

el Perú
Lima

U.S. Embassy
Consular Section Corner
Avenidas Inca Garcilaso
de la Vega and Expaña P.O.
Box 1995 Lima 1
1-51-14-33-8000-Mailing
Address:APO AA 34031

la República Dominicana
Santo Domingo

U.S. Embassy
Consular Section corner of
Caller César Nicolás
Pensón and Calle Leopoldo
Navarro
1-809-541-2171

Uruguay
Montevideo
U.S. Embassy
Consular Section Lauro Muller #1776
1-2-23-60-61
Mailing Address: APO AA34035

Venezuela
Caracas

U.S. Embassy
Consular Section Avenida Francisco de Mirand
and Avenida Principal de la Floresta
P.O. Box 62291
1-2-285-3111/2222
Mailing Address: APO AA 34037

Improving

Spanish

Computer Web Sites
of
Enrichment

Recommended

LEARNING SPANISH ONLINE

Learning Basic Spanish Online - All are Free Sites – The ones in *RED* are very good sites. The *Blue* sites move into the Advanced scene. The best site for most any academic Spanish study is the site in ***BLACK***. Enjoy and Learn-*Diviértete y Aprende*

http://www.learn-to-speaker.com/Spanish/default.htm

http://www.spanishromance.com/spanish-language/lyrics/

http://www.spaleon.com

http://www.elemadrid.com/spanish_verbs.htm

http://globegate.utm.edu/spanish/span.html

http://www.alsolnet.com/stream/argentinagayradio

http://www.spanishpronto.com/spanishpronto/index.html

http://www.learn-to-speaker.com/Spanish/default.htm

http://www.mcps.k12.md.us/schools/wjhs/mediactr/forlangpathfinder/famhisp4/famhis4.html

http://www.freetranslation.com/free

http://www.mansioningles.com/Vocabulario.htm

LEARNING SPANISH ONLINE

Learning Basic Spanish Online - All are Free Sites – The ones in *RED* are very good sites. The *Blue* sites move into the Advanced scene. The best site for most any academic Spanish study is the site in ***BLACK***. Enjoy and Learn-*Diviértete y Aprende*

http://www.personal.psu.edu/faculty/c/s/csr4/PSU3/Hispanic-Latino-Americans/Hispanic-Latino-Americans.html

http://coloquio.com/famosos/alpha.html

http://www.uni.edu/becker/Spanish3.html

http://www.spanishromance.com/spanish-language/lyrics/

http://noticias.espanol.yahoo.com

http://www.telemundo.com/index.html

http://babelfish.altavista.com

MACHISMO

The Misunderstanding of the

MACHO man

with the gay flare!

Understanding -Masculinity and Culture-crossing all ethic barriers, living lies, surpressed desires Machismo, hombres y machos-lo bueno, lo malentendido y lo oscuro; deseos contenidos y doble vidas

Terms for understanding from the Latino Spanish which may help in comprehending the 'male' mindset

1. **Calzones** Basically means 'shorts' or 'underwear', regardless of gender. Someone who "wears the pants" or the strong/dominate person in a relationship.

2. **Conquista** The ultimate conquest of the stronger, usually the male/macho person over the weaker and or one who submits (by choice or not) to the stronger or dominant.

3. **Hembra** In the primal since of the word, the one being dominated by the more powerful or stronger and the one who is being bred; generally the female/woman and not referring to the word 'feminine'. Hembra also has the understanding and connotation of and or implying a strong woman, internal strength as well as exhibiting an outward control.

4. **Joto** Queer, with negative implications; a receiver, one who is being penetrated by a dominant figure, who may consider himself 'straight', not necessarily homosexual; with implications of a 'female' role, while being 'normal' in his sexual experience. Joto is offensive and many times is used to degrade and is often times used as an expression of power or dominance. In most languages of the world the term 'gay' does not have a translation equivalent and is a non offensively acceptable and widely used.

5. **Macho**   Wow, a very difficult word to define but is of a primal origin. Taken from expression 'he mule' or 'he goat'. "Macho" being used to differentiate between 'female'/hembra in the breeding process and the 'male'/macho, as the breeder and dominant one as to the 'female'/as member, the one who being dominated or bred. There are a variety of connotations and denotations for "Macho" which will unfold and will give more understanding to the complex and misused term.

6. **Machismo** As complex as the human animal; many times misunderstood and an overly exaggerated since of being male/manly/masculine and many times expressing "chauvinism" both the positive qualities, and expressing the negative attributes of 'man;' the naked animal. Generally 'machismo' has and exhibits unacceptable attributes of qualities associated with men and or being a gentleman. Most believe that to be a man is to possess sexual equipment for reproduction and the total primal qualities of dominance and power to reproduce offspring. This may have had merit, but not in the world of today. "Man" has for the most part elevated himself to a higher level, or at least we hope.

7. **Maricón/Marica** Many times associated with the effeminate and or 'girly', 'sissy'; almost synonymous with homosexual. Looking at the word one may see Maria/Mary a term used within the homosexual communities; Mary/Maria, which may also connote femininity.

8. Puto   Many times is used as Joto, but has a literal meaning of 'male whore'. The word is used to insult, to degrade and to offend. The term Joto crosses many barriers of sex, homosexual or heterosexual, a person who receive money for sexual favors, regardless of being active homosexually or heterosexually as well as being passive homosexually.

9. Activo/Pasivo/Versatil   Top, Bottom, Versatile. To be **Top** in the homosexual community may have different connotations. Some suggest that the active may involve himself as the dominant/power person while engaging in fellatio, having himself serviced, and maybe a mutual fellatio, the one penetrating and yes, there maybe caressing, hugging, fondling and even some kissing, but with major emphasis on penetrating the submissive passive person.

The **Bottom** person may enjoy the all the above but their main emphasis is to be penetrated. Being **Versatile** is enjoying both roles. As well as this three roles is also the **Oral** preference with their major emphasis only the oral pleasures that the he enjoys with little interest in the of sexual adventure as a Active-Top/Passive-Bottom and or Versatile person.

Now, on the other hand in the heterosexual community, there are many men, and according to much research around 30% of married men enjoy the fruits of homosexual relations without classifying nor admitting to themselves as being homosexual. Most engage in the active role and for what many researchers state, will only play the role of the 'macho'/breeder/dominant/power figure, the penetrator and the one who enjoys having himself serviced; and in the same breath, refuses to admit 'deviancy' or practicing homosexual relations; and that there is nothing wrong with this practice; a double life, a suppressed desires, a life of lies to his female partner.

What is positive about being 'macho'?

According to many, 'macho' is a form of being masculine, manly with qualities of courage, honor, respect, pride, humility, responsibility, valor and going beyond the call of duty. However, these qualities maybe found crossing all genders, maybe quixotic by nature, but this is also debatable as with many of the stated qualities.

Courage:
Honor:
Respect:
Pride:
Humility:
Responsibility
Valor:
Quixotic, a gentleman, the knight errant
A leader
A man of love and compassion
Ethical
Sincerity
Belief and practice of fidelity

Measuring the external and internal qualities of 'machismo' are as different as night and day. Many times the external are 'too' apparent and most undesirable qualities to possess when not used in a positive fashion. There are very few qualities required to be 'manly', or 'macho', only the primal physical reproductiveness of the male animal. On the contrary, the quixotic qualities of being 'macho' are many and most assuredly positive and enriching.

It would be wonderful if the _negative qualities_ were few but they are more than one would imagine;

Uncontrollable anger

Infidelity

Loud and boisterous

Abusive

Chauvinistic

Dishonorable

Bullish

Disrespectful

Confrontational

Selfish

Cowardly

Disrespectful

Intrusive

Irresponsible

Sexually aggressive and abusive

Sexually repressed desires that are put into practice crossing all genders

Sexually Dominant and power driven

Suppress desires causing infidelity with same sex

Behavior straying from the norm

Untrustworthiness

Low self esteem, among other things…

Gay Web Sites:

There are so many gay sites on the WWW to mention and I suggest that you consult the web. For most Latino sites, just type in *gay* and the *country* (*gayspain/gaymexico*). **One of the best search engines for this is *ASK.COM* ..... *With each site you will find so much information of places to go in the cities of that country, special gay tours, gay hotels, gay friendly hotels, gay restaurants, gay bath houses, gay bars/discos, book stores, sex shops, how to meet and of course, most do include safety precautions.***

In most Spanish speaking countries, the guys are wonderful, but please be cautious. In the developing countries, and for reasons of economics, you may run into *'gay for hire'* as well as *hustlers*. Hopefully you have read the section on *Machismo* to give you a better understanding. Most will let you know up front what they are looking for and what they expect. Some must help provide for their families. I am just making you aware of some situations that you may run into, depending upon the country you are visiting, but most are not gay for hire or hustlers. In the coastal areas and resort areas, it may be more prevelent. **Always Be Careful.**

The sites listed below are sources in which you may be able to meet other people in many Spanish-speaking countries. You may know of others and that is wonderful; these are just a few suggested ones. I have found them to be extremely helpful.

Gay Web Sites:

http://www.thequeeragenda.com

http://www.men4menusa.com

http://www.silverdaddies.com

http://www.men4sexnow.com

http://personals.gaydadson.com

http://www.gaydar.com

http://www.gayfriendfinder.com

http://www.gay.com

Bibliography

I must remark that during my quest to finalize this book, much was acquired from many sources, the world wide web, gay chat rooms but most were people that I had met, both men, young men, boys, adventurous women, as well as Latin lovers that I have had in my lifetime. During my travels to Spain and Latin America many interviews were conducted that helped enrich and broaden my understanding of "colorful" Spanish language. Also, when I was uncertain of expressions, I would ask my friends on the web in chat rooms as well as those that I had met during my travels and my Latino friends in the States. The books that I have listed below also greatly gave me the opportunity to develop ad different perspective of the Latino mindset.

Hombres Y Machos. Masculinity and Latino Culture by Alfredo Mirande
University of California at Riverside, Westview Press. 1998
(Read the entire book, but focus attention to chapters 5 and 6.)

Chapero Viene de Chupa by Jaime Naulart,
Collección Erosman
Barcelona, España 1999
(If you read Spanish, this is a great book that opens your eyes to 'hustling' in Spain.

The author and acknowledgements

After thirty plus years teaching high school and college Spanish, there are many things that have not been taught at those levels. Remember how frustrating it was wondering how to say words and phrases about sex, and especially gay sex? So, I decided to compile this book just for you so,b you do not have to wonder any more! This book will include just about everything that you have ever wanted to know and much, much more! A great percent of the book was written on my travels to the many Spanish speaking countries and through interviews with countless native speakers. Gay, of course!

I have been to Spain four times spending weeks upon weeks in most all of the provinces. Over the past 35 years my travels to Latin America have been more extensive, living and studying in Mexico for over a year with over 40 return trips to most of the entire country exploring the enriching culture of our neighbors to ours southern boarder. Within the past 15 years, I have explored the colorful, cultural riches of Guatemala spending months with the gualtemaltecos.

I have also had the pleasure of three fantastic, magical adventures to Peru, which were truly spiritual experiences that enlightened and enriched me greatly. Other Spanish speaking countries that I have traveled and explored are Puerto Rico, Costa Rica, Panama, Bolivia, Brazil, Uruguay and yes, Argentina.

I wish to thank many friends and colleagues for their encouragement to write this book. They have read my work and have given me many helpful suggestions to finalize the process.

Much thanks to all the people that I met during my travels and the many friends in Mexico, Guatemala, Peru and Argentina that I made over the years.
Mil Gracias!

A special thank you to my friend at the Universidad de Puebla, México for his time and efforts in helping with this venture.

Gracias a Todos.

jonathan l. charles